SILENCE
AND
NOISE

SILENCE
AND
NOISE

GROWING UP ZEN IN AMERICA

IVAN RICHMOND

ATRIA BOOKS

NEW YORK LONDON TORONTO SYNDEY SINGAPORE

ATRIA BOOKS
1230 Avenue of the Americas
New York, NY 10020

ISBN: 0-7434-1755-0

First Atria Books trade paperback edition July 2003

10   9   8   7   6   5   4   3   2   1

ATRIA   BOOKS is a trademark of Simon & Schuster, Inc.

Designed by Joseph Rutt

All photos courtesy of the author

Manufactured in the United States of America

For information regarding special discounts for bulk purchases,
please contact Simon & Schuster Special Sales at 1-800-456-6798
or business@simonandschuster.com

*To all the people who have ever lived at Green Gulch
and ever will live at Green Gulch, and to all Buddhists
of the past, present, and future*

ACKNOWLEDGMENTS

Thank you to my agent, Eileen Cope, and her associate Dorian Karchmar, of Lowenstein-Yost Assoc., to my editors, Tracy Behar and Wendy Walker, to Mel Weitsman Sojan Roshi, abbot of the Berkeley Zen Center, to Judith Kern, to my father, Lewis Richmond, to my mother, Amy Richmond, and to my dear friend Noah Fischer for their suggestions, information, and insights.

CONTENTS

WHO I AM

I am not like most Westerners. I don't always recognize cultural references. I see the world differently from most of the people I know. I am patient. I try to see the silver lining in adversity. I've never been to a rock concert and have no desire to go. At the time of this writing, I'm still twenty-seven years old.

As I've entered my adult life, I've pondered deeply what it is that makes me different and what is the nature of that difference. I'm on a quest to understand my roots and determine how my upbringing, background, and life experiences have affected me and my perception of the world.

When I told a woman at work that I, a Caucasian American, was raised Buddhist, she asked, "Is that possible?" It is possible. When I was born, in 1974, my parents were members of the San Francisco Zen Center, the first Zen Buddhist monastery established in America. According to my father, its founder, Shunryu Suzuki, came to San Francisco from Japan in 1959 to be the head priest of Sokoji Japanese Buddhist Temple in San Francisco, where he led a congregation of Japanese Americans. By the mid-sixties, many Western students began practicing Zen meditation with him at the temple. They did not as a rule intermingle with the Japanese congregation, because they were given their own space that was not used by the Japanese congregation. In 1967, Suzuki and his Western students founded Tassajara as a monastery and retreat center. He taught Buddhism both in Tassajara and in San Francisco.

Then, in 1969, the San Francisco temple was becoming too crowded. The Japanese congregation complained that the temple really had two congregations, theirs and the Western group. So, the Western group bought an old residence club for Jewish women in San Francisco and converted it into the San Francisco Zen Center (referred to informally by the congregation as the City Center).

My father had been ordained a priest in 1971 by Suzuki, who became something of an icon—however un-Buddhist that may sound—among American Buddhists. Although I knew my father only as a Buddhist priest, Buddhism was not his native religion. He was raised in Riverside, California, near Los Angeles, and, after graduating from Harvard in 1967, he went directly into a Unitarian seminary in Berkeley. In 1968, he became involved with a seminary field study of the Zen groups then emerging in Berkeley and San Francisco. By the end of that year, he'd left the seminary and joined up with Suzuki's meditation group in Berkeley, and later moved to the center in San Francisco.

My mother, who had been teaching at the San Francisco

Hearing and Speech Center, became interested in Buddhism when she went to the Zen group with my father. I have always known her as a Buddhist layperson.

For the first three years of my life, we lived in an apartment next to the Zen Center building in San Francisco. People came to the large brick building as they would to a church—to meditate, chant, and practice Japanese Zen Buddhism.

Shunryu Suzuki Roshi (roshi is a Zen title equivalent to that of abbot) died in 1971, and in 1977 we moved to the newest branch of the Zen Center, Green Gulch Farm, a self-contained Zen monastery near Muir Beach, just north of San Francisco. In 1972, after Suzuki's death, the Zen Center purchased some land in Muir Beach, California, from a wealthy landowner named George Wheelwright, who was one of the cofounders of Polaroid. Green Gulch comprises eighty acres of land, including an organic farm and housing for the many monks and laypeople who want to devote their lives to the study and practice of Zen Buddhism. At the age of three-and-a-half, I began life in the monastery with my parents.

We occupied half a house close to the zendo (the meditation hall) that we shared with another family. The entire community of about fifty people ate in the communal dining room, and I lived in close community with other children.

My world was full of chanting, the reverberation of gongs beating out the rhythm of the monks' days, and bells invoking their meditation. The air I breathed was scented with sandalwood incense. Green Gulch was filled with the ritualistic, deliberate emptiness of silence. It was my only home and my only world. Although I was aware, as a child, of the outside world and did occasionally enter the American milieu, I always came home to Green Gulch.

Then, when I was ten years old, my parents moved out. At that time, I crossed a bridge so fast that I barely knew I'd crossed it. Suddenly, I found myself living entirely in that other milieu. Where Green Gulch had been a world of meditation, simplicity, and silence, America, to me, was a world of mania, excess, and noise. I've always called this other world "America," even though Green Gulch was part of it, because to me America means "the outside."

One purpose for my writing this book is simply to state, "I am a second-generation American Buddhist, and people like me do exist." If all American Buddhists were converts, like my parents, we wouldn't really have American Buddhism; we'd just have a counterculture. But the fact that there are second-generation American Buddhists means that Buddhism is now part of the American culture, however small a part that might be. For that reason, I hope that any of you who are interested in Buddhism and who want to understand it as a new American tradition will also be interested in and benefit from learning about my life. If you do, then perhaps by writing about my own experiences I may, in some small way, be contributing to the future of that tradition.

In order to understand what it has meant for me to be an American Buddhist, you must first understand me on a personal level. How has my Buddhism affected my view of life and the world? What tensions rivet my psyche into the alignment it has? What does it mean to have left behind the world I grew up in, and how do I now react to American culture?

What is it about my psychological makeup as a born-and-raised Buddhist in America that has caused me to react as I have both to the American world and to the converts who paved the way for my being? How do I finally emerge in the present as an American Buddhist? And so, in the end, it is my whole life I will need to share with you.

When we left Green Gulch, my parents were simply returning to the culture in which they'd been raised. I, however, became an immigrant in a foreign land. I was thrust into a foreign culture with very little support and no safety net. Since that time, my life has been filled with tensions and conflicts, and it's those conflicts, as well as how I've come to live with and resolve them, that have shaped my identity. Sometimes I've been tempted by the desire to have all the things Americans have, but that I was denied at Green Gulch. And then my inner pendulum will swing back again to the Buddhist values I was raised with. At times I've been confronted with the expectations people in America have of me, and I've had to reconcile those expectations with my own Buddhist values and culture. Doing this means living with an ongoing inner tug-of-war between the Buddhist ways of Green Gulch and the foreign ways of America.

Fortunately, Buddhism itself has come to my aid in this struggle. Buddhist doctrines abound with phrases like, "Form is emptiness; emptiness is form," and "Delusions are inexhaustible; I vow to end them." These apparently paradoxical statements are fundamental to Zen Buddhist philosophy. In Buddhism, we don't attach to opposites and, therefore, we don't get caught in contradictions. If we are not caught by opposites or contradictions, then perhaps my conflicts aren't really conflicts.

There's a classic paradox in Western philosophy that revolves around smashing a vase. You have a ceramic vase and then you smash it. Since all the pieces are there, did you really destroy the vase? A Buddhist would answer that the ceramic vase was originally a lump of clay that, presumably, came out of a larger lump of clay. The clay was formed into the shape of a vase, was fired, and became a vase. Then it was smashed. Nothing ceased to exist. However you refer to it, the material existed the entire time. The existence of the vase is an illusion, because we think there is a difference between unmolded, unfired clay, a ceramic vase, and ceramic shards, but, in reality, there is not. So there is no existence and no nonexistence. To a Buddhist, this is perfectly logical.

As I've encountered conflicts between Buddhist culture and American culture, I've been able to use Buddhist understanding like this to help me. It would be easy to view the tension between my two worlds as irresolvable, and it's sometimes difficult to see past the apparent conflicts in order to end the ongoing war in my mind between sets of opposites. Over time, however, I've come to understand that the sets of opposites inside me can exist harmoniously, like the two halves of the yin yang, swirling around one another.

One concept central to Buddhist teaching is the concept of the Middle Way. The Buddha experienced many extremes in his life before he became enlightened. He experienced what it was like to be extremely wealthy and extremely poor. He experienced extreme materialism and extreme asceticism. But it was not until he finally became enlightened that he realized

we have to live in balance between extremes. He taught that while it was not good to be a slave to one's desires, it was also not good to deny oneself one's basic needs. He called this balance the Middle Way.

Finding the Middle Way has been at the core of my efforts to resolve the conflicts between Buddhist culture and American culture that permeate my life. I've sometimes felt as if I were being pulled apart by two sets of extremes, and for a long time I thought I had to choose between the ways of Green Gulch and the ways of America. But I've finally figured out that it is actually possible for me to find a Middle Way.

In Buddhism, we have a hand position called "the jewel-holding mudra." A mudra is a type of hand gesture that symbolizes some aspect of Buddhist philosophy. You've probably seen statues of the Buddha making a variety of hand gestures, such as touching his forefinger and thumb together or touching the earth. These are mudras. We make the jewel-holding mudra by putting our hands together in front of our heart. It looks kind of like we're praying, but the gesture actually symbolizes two opposites becoming one. We imagine that between our hands is a jewel. The jewel is enlightenment, because true enlightenment comes from seeing beyond the opposites.

Meditation is one tool we can use to bring our consciousness to an understanding of the oneness of opposites. In Zen meditation, we practice not thinking. We try to clear our minds of all thought. When I meditate, I sit on a zafu (a meditation cushion) and cross my legs. If I can, I try to put one or both my feet over my thighs in the lotus position. I breathe in and out slowly. I smell the aroma of sandalwood incense.

The beginning of a meditation session is signaled by the ringing of a special bell whose sound fades very slowly. I listen to the sound of the bell until I can't hear it anymore. Then I start to count my breaths from one to ten, and when I get to ten, I start over at one—it's harder than you think to not think about anything. Thoughts come unbidden. If nothing else, I'll inevitably think, "Am I thinking?" and then I realize that that counts as a thought. But, it's hard to think when you're concentrating on counting your breaths, and that's the idea. After I do this for a while, my head clears and I get to a point, even for just a moment or two, when I'm not thinking about anything at all.

When I meditate, all the opposites go away. I realize that what I think of as contradictions are not contradictory. I can't describe in words what that's like, because the moment I start thinking about it, I interrupt my meditation. But, somehow, the war in my soul between Buddhist culture and American culture gets silenced. The sets of opposites cease to be in conflict. I can hold one in each hand and bring them together in the jewel-holding mudra.

It's likely that everything you, or anyone else, has heard or read about Buddhism until now has come from an American convert or from an Asian Buddhist who brought his native religion to America. Therefore, I would like to share my own views with you. Some people (Buddhists in particular) might say I'm not enlightened enough yet, and perhaps I'm not. However, I think that someone of my generation and my identity can offer a unique, and therefore useful, perspective on American Buddhism.

There's not much sense in America of what it means to be just a normal, everyday, rank-and-file Buddhist—the Buddhist equivalent of a Christian who goes to church on Sunday or a Jew who goes to synagogue on Saturday, but who probably hasn't studied the holy books of his religion as well as has his minister, priest, or rabbi. Unless he's extremely religious, he probably doesn't spend a majority of his time at church or synagogue. He's not a monk and certainly doesn't live in a cloister. He probably doesn't even follow the rules all the time. He probably strays from his beliefs with some degree of frequency but has a priest or minister or rabbi to talk to if he's in need of counseling. That's the kind of Buddhist I see myself as being.

I'm not a master or a teacher. My parents' own teacher, Shunryu Suzuki, allowed his students to publish a book of his talks entitled *Zen Mind, Beginner's Mind.* Since then, many Buddhists from other countries and Buddhist immigrants like Suzuki have published their teachings on American presses. And it was not long before the converts, too, achieved a level of mastery that allowed them to publish as well. They all have a lot of wisdom to share.

Even so, Buddhist writing has generally been considered countercultural. The writers have been either immigrants or converts. And they were writing for converts and other people interested in incorporating Buddhism into their spirituality or psychology. In a word, Western Buddhist writing, up to now, has been written by converts for converts.

I am not one of those writers. Being a second-generation American Buddhist is an identity separate from being either an immigrant or a convert. And I think the Buddhists of my generation need a voice of our own. Even though I'm not a teacher, there are some things I think I can teach.

Buddhist converts ought to know about me because I'm the next generation. Non-Buddhists need to know about me because I represent a new American religion. Americans should know about me because my identity, in a way, redefines some small aspect of American culture.

Therefore, I believe it's time in the history of American Buddhism to write a new sort of book, not a book by a foreign Buddhist master nor a work by an American Buddhist teacher, but a teaching from the experiences of a foot soldier in the new generation. The ideas in this book were not derived from study or meditation but rather from my life as a whole. It's time for my generation to speak.

ONE

AN AMERICAN IMMIGRANT IN AMERICA— EIGHT CONFLICTS

THE WORLD OF GREEN GULCH

I have lived in two worlds. One is the world of Green Gulch. Green Gulch was a world landscaped with religion. The fields were religious with the practice of simplicity. The dining room was religious with the purity of our meals—brown rice, tofu, and organic produce from our farm. The paths to the zendo were religious with silence.

Ours was a religion in which the emptiness of delusion was discouraged and the full wealth of enlightenment was what we sought. By enlightenment, I simply mean a deep and profound understanding of life and of what was truly important in life, such as birth, death, loving others, the good of the world, the arts, and inner beauty. We at Green Gulch didn't think we were enlightened, but Buddhists believe that the Buddha was enlightened. In Buddhism, we don't believe that enlighten-

My father and I on the porch of the Bullpens. Like most Buddhist monks and priests, he keeps his head shaved and wears robes.

ment is necessarily easy to achieve, but we also believe that it is an ever-approachable perfection.

The Buddha taught the Four Noble Truths, which, as I was told them, say that all human beings suffer; that suffering is caused by desire; that the key to avoiding suffering is to avoid desire; and that we can avoid desire by achieving enlightenment. Delusion, then, which is the opposite of enlightenment, is caused by the desire for things that prevent one from understanding what's truly important in life, which are, in the simplest of terms, material goods and possessions.

At Green Gulch, we tried to live in a way that would bring us closer and closer to the enlightenment of the Buddha, and to stay away from any delusions that would derail us from that path.

As children, we learned from the role-modeling of the adults not to display intemperate emotions, such as anger or overexcitement, but to be meditative at all times, to live a simple life, free from consumerism and materialism, and to avoid the temptations to delusion that are found in popular culture.

Of the fifty or so people who lived at Green Gulch, most were monks or laypeople. Buddhism has traditionally been based on student/teacher relationships. A teacher helps the student to achieve enlightenment by teaching him or her Buddhist philosophy. At Green Gulch, the students might be either monks or laypeople. The monks were people who had been ordained by a Buddhist priest and who had dedicated their lives to practicing Buddhism as a profession. Unlike monks of the Catholic religion, Zen Buddhist monks in America are not necessarily required to be celibate, and are free to marry. They do, however, take sixteen vows, similar to the Ten Commandments, that guide their behavior. I reproduce them here exactly as the monk taking them would speak them:

> I take refuge in the Buddha.
> I take refuge in the Dharma.
> I take refuge in the Sangha.
> I vow to refrain from all evil.
> I vow to do good.
> I vow to live to benefit all beings.
> A disciple of the Buddha does not willfully take life.
> A disciple of the Buddha does not take what is not given.
> A disciple of the Buddha does not engage in sexual misconduct.
> A disciple of the Buddha does not lie.
> A disciple of the Buddha does not intoxicate oneself or others.
> A disciple of the Buddha does not slander.
> A disciple of the Buddha does not praise self at the expense of others.
> A disciple of the Buddha is not spiritually or materially avaricious.
> A disciple of the Buddha does not bear ill will.
> A disciple of the Buddha does not ignore Buddha, Dharma, Sangha, their own enlightened nature.

The word "Dharma" refers to the teachings of the Buddha. The Sangha can mean the congregation, all Buddhists, or all people in the world. The phrase, "a disciple of the Buddha," is just a fancy way of saying a Buddhist monk or in America, a layperson. Even though a Buddhist monk is literally the disciple of his teacher, he is also, figuratively, a disciple of the Buddha himself, because the Buddha's teachings are still "alive" through the written word of the sutras and the teachings of Buddhist teachers.

In addition to taking these vows, monks wear robes and shave their heads. Each monk also has a special bowl called an oryoki that, at least at Green Gulch, they used to eat meals in the zendo during long meditation sessions. All the monks were expected to live on campus.

At Green Gulch, the laypeople were members of the congregation who had not received monastic ordination or taken monastic vows. They didn't shave their heads or wear robes, but they wore a rectangular cloth called a rakusu that hangs from the neck. They were not required to live at Green Gulch, but many chose to do so, either out of dedication to Buddhism or because, like my mother, they were married to monks.

The priests were monks who, like my father, held a higher rank in the community than that of an ordinary monk. Priests might be compared to the clergy in Western religions. They are leaders of the congregation who have the ability to train monks and laypeople and give them ordination. They conduct religious ceremonies and services, are licensed to perform marriages, and also preside at funerals.

Although these definitions may vary somewhat from one congregation to another, they were the ones that prevailed at Green Gulch.

Most of the monks and laypeople lived in a two-story wooden dormitory adjacent to the zendo called the gaitan. In traditional Japanese Zen monasteries, the gaitan is not generally the same as the monks' quarters. It is the lobby just outside of the zendo. At Green Gulch, however, our gaitan was housed in our dormitory, so we referred to the entire building as the gaitan. It had two main entrances with screen doors. One door allowed access to the gaitan from the area surrounding a complex known as the Wheelwright Center (named after the man from whom Green Gulch's land had been purchased). The Wheelwright Center was comprised of two two-story buildings. The second stories of these buildings were joined by one big deck called the Upper Deck that allowed you to walk from the upper-story room of one building to the upper-story room of the other.

One of these buildings housed guest rooms on the lower level. On the upper level was a lecture room, which was also used for social events. The other building contained the dining room and kitchen on the lower floor, as well as a small annex called the family room. The upper story housed the library.

If you walked through the other door out of the gaitan, you would come to a grassy lawn that we called the Central Area, where the community often gathered. To one side of the Central Area was the post office. It wasn't an official United States post office, but it was where our mail was delivered. Mainly, it was used as an administrative office, and if someone called Green Gulch's main telephone number, he would get the post office. The hills surrounding the gulch rose above the gaitan, the Wheelwright Center, and the Central Area.

Some of the monks and laypeople in our community were married and had children. Those with families didn't live in the gaitan but in trailers and tiny houses nestled among the valley's golden grasses. Each house and trailer had several tiny bedrooms, a small kitchen, an equally small bathroom, and a basic living area.

Although, as I've said, we at Green Gulch didn't think of ourselves as enlightened, we did try—as best we were able—to live according to Buddhist precepts. We tried to avoid the pitfalls that come with desire. We didn't want to eat fancy food, live in big houses, or drive fancy cars. We didn't want to fill our heads with television or loud music. We didn't try to forget the reality of our lives by acquiring expensive but unnecessary luxuries. We believed in having just what we needed, eating food that nurtured us, and paying attention to the things that are really important. We believed in being quiet so that our minds could be quiet. When our minds were filled with silence, we could almost hear ourselves living. Then, in those moments of inner silence, we could find happiness in the things that enrich us and take pleasure in simply being alive.

THE WORLD OUTSIDE

The "outside"—America—was viewed by the people of Green Gulch as the world of the unenlightened, slaves to the delusions of their society and culture. Outside, people were thought to be intemperate. Their minds, we were led to believe, were cluttered with empty ambitions and materialistic desires. In effect, we were taught to think of the world outside as the opposite of Green Gulch in every respect.

While I imagine that, to some degree, every religion and even every political or social group perceives itself to be superior to the "outside," the important difference to understand here is that Green Gulch and the outside were separate worlds. We children went into the outside world five times a week to attend school, but we played almost exclusively with one another and seldom, if ever, with children whose parents were not in some way affiliated with the Zen Center. We tasted the fruits of the outside only in contrast to our own flavors.

A BUDDHIST IMMIGRANT IN AMERICA

Leaving Green Gulch was, for me, like crossing a psychological border. Once we left, my mind and soul were in foreign territory. However, like all immigrants, I brought my "native" culture with me, a culture that defines me still. Just as an immigrant from China, for example, leaves China, enters America, and becomes a Chinese American, so I left Green Gulch, entered America, and today I am an American Buddhist.

In the outside world, I soon discovered, people judged me by standards that were completely the opposite of those I'd been raised with—such as how I dressed and how much money my parents made. For the first time, I was tantalized by things that had always been remote from my way of life— candy bars, Saturday morning cartoons, and popular toys such as action figures. At the time, all these things seemed really exciting. I was still a kid, after all, and at first I binged on everything I'd been denied at Green Gulch. It seemed decadent and outrageous. But I also had a nagging feeling in the pit of my stomach that something was wrong with it all. It was *too* good. My parents, however, did almost nothing to help me to learn how to live in this new world *without* bingeing. Later on, I would have to discover on my own how to live in America and still be true to myself.

As a cultural being, I am comprised of polar opposites. My psyche is filled with things Green Gulch and things American. These associations are set one against the other as us versus them, near versus far, native versus foreign, same versus other, old versus new, yin versus yang. Green Gulch culture is, for me, a thesis, and American culture its antithesis.

Much of the Judeo-Christian tradition, I have noticed, involves identifying and separating opposites—good from evil, thou shalts from thou shalt nots, for example. Let's just talk for a moment about Light and Dark. Good, God, Heaven, God's commandments, and God's worshipers are all in the category of Light. Evil, the Devil, Hell, sin, and those who don't worship God are all in the category of Dark. Light is preferred over Dark. Light is to be had and held alone, apart from Dark. A good person is supposed to hold the Light only. Darkness needs the Light to illuminate and expose it. Anyone who holds to Darkness is bad. Now, let's add to the category of Light the terms familiar, us, near, same, and related concepts. To Dark then we add foreign, them, far, other, etc.

In Buddhism, we believe that a truly enlightened person doesn't separate opposites. We try to hold opposites like Light and Dark in both hands, one pole in each. The Light is not always good and the Dark is not always bad. I'm not enlightened, however, and too often I still fall into the trap of seeing Green Gulch and America as opposites. But, ever since leaving Green Gulch, I've been trying to find a way to hold in one hand the culture of Green Gulch and in the other the culture of America. If I can do that, and then bring my two hands together, I've got something else: me, now. I have my own culture today, which is comprised of my immigrant's culture and the culture I brought with me from Green Gulch.

Within me there are many conflicts formed by the fact that, culturally speaking, I'm both Buddhist and American. Who I am today is paramount and pivotal to an understanding of American Buddhism, but who I am cannot be understood without first understanding the opposites that form my identity. To do this, we need to explore these conflicts.

LEAVING GREEN GULCH: THE FIRST CONFLICT

Knowing how different the world of Green Gulch was from traditional American culture, it shouldn't be difficult to understand what a shock it was when my parents took me, at the age of ten, out of the environment in which I'd grown up and thrust me into a new and virtually foreign land—the land I call America. It's likely that none of the other contradictions or conflicts in my life ever would have occurred if my parents hadn't taken me to live at Green Gulch in the first place, or, more importantly, if we'd never left. But we did.

I had always known my father as a Buddhist priest and an important member of our community. My mother I knew as a

devout Buddhist layperson. Together, they had always epito-
mized our simple lifestyle. To me, then, leaving seemed totally
at odds with everything I knew them to be. All they told me, by
way of explanation for their decision, was that they had spent
close to fifteen years practicing Buddhism and they felt that
was long enough to study it so intensely. Now they wanted to
move on. I didn't want to leave, but, clearly, it wasn't up to me.

It all happened so quickly that, at the time, I was barely
able to process the enormity of the change. I realized, of
course, that I was living in a very different place in very different circumstances, and that suddenly many things that had
been forbidden became accessible. But now, as I look back on
it, I realize there could hardly have been a more profound
change in my life.

For my parents it was different. They were *of* America.
They'd grown up in it. They'd rebelled against it, and they'd
found Buddhism. Leaving Green Gulch was, for them, returning to their native country, so to speak. It was a place they already knew well, and even when I talk to them now, they don't
entirely understand how foreign American culture appeared to
me. They think of themselves as Americans and never thought
of me as being any different. I guess, to them I was just at
Green Gulch because it was where they were currently living.

But Green Gulch was my life and my world. Being a Buddhist was my identity. And, as far as I was concerned, it was
theirs, too. It was a world they'd found and founded. It was
where they'd decided to raise me. How could they so suddenly
separate me—and themselves—from that life?

My parents remained nominally Buddhist. They still had
their zafus, and they kept an altar in our new house. They

meditated sporadically and in private, but they didn't join a congregation. We very seldom talked about Buddhism after we left, and I didn't understand that either. How could we not talk about it when I'd seen, heard, and smelled it all around me for as long as I could remember? To me, it made no sense.

I don't want to sound entirely self-centered. I believe in enlightenment, and so I've given a lot of thought to what the Green Gulch experience had been from my parents' perspective. I realize that Buddhism wasn't what they'd been raised with. I understand that Green Gulch was simply a place where they'd decided, as adults, to live a portion of their lives. They invested their lives from 1969 until 1984 in Zen Buddhism at the Zen Center—years that spanned three decades. And what I still don't understand is how they could so suddenly just put it all away and start a new life as a nuclear family in their own, private house in small-town suburbia.

Certainly, as an adult, I've asked them about this, and I'll talk about their reasons—or the reasons they've given me—at greater length in the following chapter. For now, I just want to make clear what an enormous change their decision made in my life, and how it has led to the many other conflicts I've been trying to resolve ever since.

BUDDHIST CULTURE VERSUS POPULAR CULTURE: THE SECOND CONFLICT

The Buddha, as I've said, taught that desire is the root of all suffering. He said we should, therefore, avoid becoming too attached to *things*. At Green Gulch, we didn't believe in following popular culture because we considered adhering to popular trends a form of attachment. We thought that being interested in or involved with something simply *because* it was popular would enslave us and mire us in delusion.

By contrast, American culture is full of all sorts of popular icons, such as rock stars, movie stars, and sports stars. There are movies everyone goes to and movies that are considered classics. There are television shows everyone watches, and TV, too, has its classics. As an American, one is expected to be familiar with these elements of popular culture.

American society presents people with a kind of social in/out list, comparable to the lists in magazines that summarize what's currently "in" or "out" of favor. There's certainly nothing inherently wrong with watching an entertaining movie to unwind after a long week of work. There's nothing wrong with appreciating the arts, and everyone has the right to decide what he or she considers "art" or "literature." But if you're a slave to society's in/out lists, you're not making that determination for yourself, and, according to Buddhism, you're bound to something superficial and delusory. I was taught that being free from such bonds would allow me to find pleasure for myself and would empower me to create my own happiness.

The problem for me is that I was raised in a world that discouraged me from even *knowing* anything about popular culture. Not only did I not adhere to society's in/out lists, I didn't even know what was in and what was out. At Green Gulch I didn't need to know these things because Green Gulch culture didn't have in/out lists. But in America one can't really survive very well without at least some understanding of popular trends. Ever since I left Green Gulch, part of me has tried to stay away from popular culture, but I've encountered all sorts of conflicts trying to do this. When I was younger, not knowing much about popular culture made it hard to get along with my peers in America, and part of me really *wanted* everything American pop culture had to offer. For a long time I've struggled to figure out how to live in American culture and not be a slave to society's in/out lists.

NONMATERIALISM VERSUS MATERIALISM: THE THIRD CONFLICT

Materialism is directly related to popular culture. It drives the popular world. If a good Buddhist is not to be a slave to popular culture, he or she must first be free from desire for material goods. The Heart Sutra, a primary text of Zen Buddhism, states, "form is emptiness and emptiness is form." This means that the material things we believe to have value in life, such as fancy cars, large homes, or elaborate sound systems, are, in fact, emptier than we think, and that nonmaterial things, such as love and friendship, are full, deep, and rich.

Sometimes we think that form is full and emptiness empty. We think that emptiness needs to be filled. But Zen teaches that emptiness is sometimes fuller than material fullness. I've always taken this as the enlightened view of the world, and for a long time, as I've wandered my new world, I've wondered why other people didn't see this as enlightenment.

At Green Gulch, we believed strongly, as that line from the Heart Sutra implies, that material possessions couldn't really make us happy. I was taught that if I wanted a material object, I should ask myself what it was about that object that would make me happy.

For example, if I want a really expensive car, what was it about that car that I think will make me happy? If I just want to get out on the road and drive, wouldn't a less expensive car do just as well? And if I want to travel a distance, couldn't I take a train or a plane? If I want the car for status, then what I really want is status itself and not the car, and that begs the question of why I want status.

To this day I believe that material things like expensive cars can't truly make us happy. I believe the things that really make us happy are nonmaterial, such as love and friendship. From this perspective, form—in the sense of material objects—is empty of its ability to make people happy, but nonmaterial things can give us true happiness. So, I think the Heart Sutra is right. Form is emptiness. Emptiness is form.

Today, my goal in life is to be a really good writer. I don't need to be rich. So long as I have what I need—a roof over my head, food to eat, clothes to wear, enough money to pay my bills, and the things that will really make me happy, which are not material goods—I can push on with my writing and take pride in myself for pursuing what I love.

I admit, however, that the longer I've lived in what I'm calling America, the more I've become assimilated into the mainstream. I have a decent job as a computer programmer. I live in a large, one-bedroom apartment and drive a '93 car. I like to eat in restaurants and buy nice things for myself. I'm not always the perfect Buddhist. Sometimes I think material things *will* bring me pleasure, but I invariably find out that the pleasure I thought I experienced from having them was only an illusion. How to be a good, nonmaterialistic Buddhist while living in a world driven by materialism has been an ongoing conflict in my life.

PATIENCE VERSUS IMPATIENCE: THE FOURTH CONFLICT

The second of the Four Noble Truths states that suffering is caused by desire, and impatience—wishing for something to happen or trying to make it happen sooner—is certainly a form of desire. It also requires that we think too much about the future, which the Buddha taught was wrong because always thinking about the future would mean that we weren't paying enough attention to what was actually going on in the present. And for those two reasons, patience—the opposite of desire and looking to the future—is a virtue all good Buddhists ought to cultivate.

At Green Gulch, I was taught always to be patient and not to rush things because everything happens in its time. The people at Green Gulch never procrastinated, but they were also never busy or rushed. The cultural norm was to be patient because people always got the job done in whatever time they required to do it, and you could count on their not putting it off or taking longer than was necessary.

In the outside world, however, I've found that I can't always wait indefinitely for things to happen. If I'm waiting for someone to do something and I don't get impatient, there's always the chance that he or she will take advantage of my patience.

If I'm waiting for someone to call me back with the answer to a question, for example, I sometimes have to remind him or her with a second or even a third call in order to get a response. I can't simply assume that he or she is "getting the job done" in the time it naturally takes.

The pace of the world outside is so different from that of Green Gulch, and the expectations of those who live in it are so different as well, that some degree of impatience appears to be expected, if not actually necessary. American culture appears to revolve around a "squeaky wheel gets the oil" way of thinking. Americans sometimes appear to assume that if you don't nag, you're not really interested. And so, in order to survive in the outside world, I constantly have to ask myself whether to be patient or impatient in any given situation. I try to be a good Buddhist and not fall prey to desire or lose sight of the present while gazing into the future, but I also have to conform to the expectations of the world I'm now living in. Finding that balance has sometimes been difficult for me.

CHILD CARE VERSUS CHILD FREEDOM: THE FIFTH CONFLICT

Not everything at Green Gulch was ideal, or lived up to Buddhist ideology, and one aspect of my life there that I now see as far less than perfect was the way the community regarded and cared for its children. Although Buddhists are supposed to cherish children, and Buddhists elsewhere in the world believe in taking care of children, the child-care system at

Green Gulch, as I see it now, was never really adequate or well organized.

Many of the students and monks at Green Gulch didn't have kids and didn't want children around. They felt that their meditation was being interrupted by our play, and they were critical of our parents for compromising their practice in order to attend to our needs. For the most part, they tried to help us as little as possible.

Organized child care was sporadic, and the person in charge changed from month to month. We had child care through some parts of the day, but much of the time we were allowed to roam the property at will, doing whatever we wanted so long as we didn't disturb the students. There were many times when we were totally unsupervised.

Many of the adults claimed it was good for children to have a certain amount of freedom because it gave us a chance to explore the world on our own, but for me, child freedom was not a blessing.

As a result of this lack of supervision, we children were never really taught proper social skills, which made it harder for us to get along with one another (leading to the next important conflict in my life, Nonviolence versus Violence), and—even more important—we received very little formal Buddhist education. How was it possible that, as I was being raised as a new-generation member of this new tradition, no one of the previous generation cared enough to be sure I was taught its basic precepts?

In retrospect, it now seems to me that the Green Gulch community not only failed its children but also failed to live up to its Buddhist tradition. In America, children are, for the most part, given more guidance and nurturing than we received, and—at least in families where religion holds a primary position—they usually receive some sort of formal religious education.

On the other hand, despite these failings, I did learn—by whatever means—some good values that have remained important to me throughout my life. And so, I have to wonder: If it takes a village to raise a child (and Green Gulch was certainly a village), is it better to be raised by a less than perfect village than by no village at all?

NONVIOLENCE VERSUS VIOLENCE: THE SIXTH CONFLICT

Like most Buddhists, we at Green Gulch believed in pacifism. But it was a struggle for me, growing up, to reconcile my own feelings of aggression and other people's violence with my Buddhist belief in nonviolence.

The adults would scold us children for pretending to shoot guns or playing war games, but that didn't stop us from pretending to blast storm troopers when we played *Star Wars*, for instance. (Even though the Green Gulch adults disapproved of popular culture and did their best to shield us from its temptations, they were not vigilant enough—and no community could have been isolated enough—to protect us from the lure of George Lucas's epic, which was, in many ways, one of the defining events of my generation.) And because we weren't always supervised, we weren't taught how to deal with conflict when it arose among us. While all kids certainly fight, it seems to me that there was a lot more picking-on, teasing, and being mean to one another at Green Gulch than there would be in most groups of kids because, on the one hand, there was often no one around to stop us and, on the other, no one had taught us how to resolve our differences any other way.

Now, as an adult, the part of me that is a good Buddhist wants to stand up for pacifism, and, intellectually, I'm opposed to violence. I often tell myself that I'd never use violence against another person because I'm a born and raised Buddhist from Green Gulch. But, another part of me rebels at such a notion, because the adults in the community never taught us children *how* to be nonviolent toward one another. I sometimes feel that, while I was taught to embrace pacifism as a principle on an intellectual level, I never really learned to be nonviolent at the practical level. When I get angry or feel threatened, I don't always know the correct pacifist answers, so this tension continues inside me.

For most Americans, violence is bad if it's considered "evil" in someone's assessment and condoned if it's "good." In World War II, for example, America was "good" and Nazi Germany was "evil." America's use of violence was, by that logic, acceptable.

My tradition, however, categorizes acts as either enlightened or unenlightened. An enlightened person would understand that violence comes from anger and anger from fear, so that any act of violence derives from fear, and fear is unenlightened. Fear is considered unenlightened because it can be caused either by something illusory or by something real. A person might, for example, see a coil of rope and mistake it for a snake. The unenlightened person would fear the snake but the enlightened person would recognize the rope for what it was, and wouldn't fear it. Or, conversely, if the coil really were a snake, the enlightened person would recognize it as such and deal with it accordingly. In either case, the enlightened person would not be frightened.

For me, however, the question remains, how do you tell the rope from the snake? What happens when a pacifist meets someone who feels justified in using violence or aggression? What happens when a genuine pacifist meets someone who only presents a pacifist façade but is actually violent inside? And which one of these am I? I was raised a pacifist but not taught how to deal with aggression as a child. I believe in non-violence, but I also think violence is sometimes necessary. How do I resolve this dichotomy?

I continue to have many questions about nonviolence that no Buddhist teacher has ever answered to my satisfaction. What should I do if someone acts violently toward me? What if someone gets angry with me or gives me a good reason to be angry? What if I use words and people don't listen? I often wonder if pacifism is really enlightened, or if true enlightenment isn't really something that allows us to feel compassionate toward all living beings, frees us from our fears, but also allows us to protect ourselves against people who would hurt us, psychologically or physically.

EASTERN VERSUS WESTERN MORALITY: THE SEVENTH CONFLICT

Directly related to the issue of Violence versus Nonviolence is the issue of morality. Morality in Eastern philosophical traditions and throughout Eastern culture is very different from

Western concepts of morality, but not, to my mind, any less valid.

Traditionally, much of Western morality has been based on the Judeo-Christian concept of commandments or lists of thou-shalts and thou-shalt-nots, believed to have been handed down to man by God and codified in scripture.

But, in addition to Judeo-Christian morality, which is based on religion, there's also a modern perspective on morality that's espoused by those who adhere to no religion at all and who would, therefore, argue that if you have no religion, you have no way of knowing whose "commandments" to follow. If you don't know which God, if any, is the "right" or "true" God and which holy book, if any, is "authentic," how do you know which list of dos and don'ts is the "correct" one? These people would argue that it might be better not to have any do/don't list at all.

Eastern morality, however, is not based on God-given commandments or dos and don'ts lists. With all due respect to anybody who reveres a holy book that's supposed to be the word of God, in Eastern thought we believe there's a more objective way of telling right from wrong based on the concept of karma.

Karma, a Sanskrit word that literally means "action," embodies the notion that all actions have consequences. Many forms of Eastern philosophy share the belief that people need to take responsibility for their actions. Sometimes, in Eastern thought, we think of karma as a cycle or wheel of actions and reactions, and we refer to this as the Wheel of Karma.

If someone does something hurtful to you, you can either do something hurtful back or you can *not* do something hurtful back. We call the former "staying on the Wheel of Karma" or "giving the Wheel a kick," because responding in kind keeps the cycle of actions and reactions going around. We call the latter "getting off the Wheel of Karma" or "not giving the Wheel a kick," because not to respond would end the cycle of actions and reactions. In Buddhism, it is believed that one should always get off the Wheel of Karma.

The conflict for me is not whether I should adhere to an Eastern or Western concept of morality, because I firmly believe in morality based on karma. The conflict for me is how to get off the Wheel while still trying to make sure that people who do "bad" or hurtful things—that is, people who behave immorally—are made to face the consequences of their actions. Does my getting off the Wheel of Karma mean allowing another person to get away with hurting me or people I care about? Does it mean that I can't confront people who do bad things? Does it mean I can't do anything to stop people from doing bad things?

On a theoretical or philosophical level, I think I've found a way to avoid kicking the Wheel while still acting responsibly toward those I believe to be behaving immorally, and I can only hope that when I'm actually tested, I'll be able to act properly on my beliefs.

SILENCE VERSUS NOISE:
THE EIGHTH CONFLICT

Zen is just one branch of Buddhism, and in Zen we believe that the path to enlightenment is through quieting the mind. We believe it is only when we quiet our minds that we can free ourselves of desire. The Buddha didn't say we should avoid desire by being ascetic. Rather he taught something he called the Middle Way, which is a way of living that seeks a balance between two extremes—living in pursuit of desire and denying oneself the things one needs to survive. Only when we silence the noise of our own thoughts can we see this balance. And for that reason, the principal meditative practice of Zen Buddhism is to silence the mind.

The approach at Green Gulch was to keep the environment quiet so that it would be easier to keep one's mind quiet. At Green Gulch, everywhere you went it was quiet. You could walk from the dining room up a dirt road to the gaitan and from there to people's houses, and everywhere it would be tranquil.

The monks did things all day, but no one was ever busy. The loudest noise was probably that of the han (which we kids called the bopper), a hanging piece of wood that was hit rhythmically with a mallet to call people to meditation and dinner. The only other sound was that of chanting, and that was so controlled and rhythmic that it didn't sound like noise.

Out in America, however, it's almost impossible to live in silence. People hurry in every direction, in cars or on foot. Cars drive past thumping loud music. Where there was chanting in Green Gulch, on the outside there are rock concerts with cacophonous music and raucous crowds (or so I've been told).

In America, everyone of my generation expects me to understand things like rock concerts and loud music. If I say that I don't, they think something must be wrong with me. Loud music seems to match the manic fervor of American society. Everything is fast-paced and high energy, and it's almost as if

Americans need fast, loud music to keep up with it. Maybe they do. And, if they do, maybe, living in the outside world, I do, too. It's a conundrum.

But silence and noise have an even broader significance for me. To me, silence is emblematic of all the elements that define Green Gulch. Noise summarizes in one word all I associate with the rest of America. For me, they serve as the yin and yang that define these two cultures. Buddhist culture, nonmaterialism, and nonviolence belong to the world of silence. Popular culture, materialism, and violence belong in the world of noise.

But the opposition is more complicated than that. In fact, everything I associate with noise represents something that was forbidden to me at Green Gulch but is a constant temptation in America. As I've already said, I'm not yet enlightened, and I'm human in my imperfections, so that, despite my Buddhist beliefs and all my effort, as I slog down the difficult path to enlightenment, trying to live in a way that upholds those beliefs, I am still, from time to time, tempted.

Both silence and noise exist within me, and as we continue this journey, I will explore these fundamental contradictions, how they came to life inside me, and how I've learned to hold them, one in each hand, and bring them together in harmony.

TWO

LEAVING GREEN GULCH

In February 1984, my family left Green Gulch. That was without doubt the single most pivotal moment in my life. I'd lived my entire life to that point in a relatively isolated Buddhist world, and when we left, I moved into a world that was totally different. Although I must have been at least subliminally aware, even at that age, of some of the conflicts between the ideals and values with which I'd been raised and those of the world Outside, it wasn't until I began to live in that world full-time that I had to face them head-on.

For several months, my parents had been checking the newspaper and making calls, looking for a house to rent. Then, one morning in late autumn, my mother drove me into Mill Valley, the town just up the highway from Green Gulch where we'd always gone to do errands. We turned up a winding road and into a wooded valley beneath green hills. "Dad and I found a really great place out here," she told me. "It's a wonderful woodsy area and there are lots of trails and a park right nearby." As it turned out, the house they'd found was built and owned by the architect who had originally built most of the main buildings at Green Gulch.

For most of the previous year, we'd been having our dinners together at our house rather than in the community dining room. And, during that time, I'd started at a new private school. So, in a way, my life had already begun to change, but I was still coming home to the place I'd always known, and I still had the other Green Gulch kids to play with.

Perhaps I should have been more prepared than I was, and perhaps my parents should have given me a better explanation than they did, but the only explanation I got at the time was that they'd been studying Buddhism for fifteen years and now wanted to go on to lead a "normal" life. I'd always thought our life *was* normal, but apparently they didn't.

My last dinner at Green Gulch was in the dining room, where I sat with my family at one end of a long table. At the end of the meal, one of the Zen students stood up and banged a spoon against his glass. "I'd like to make an announcement," he said. "Lew, Amy, and their son, Ivan, are leaving Green Gulch tomorrow, so all of us have gotten housewarming gifts for them."

My mother put a hand to her heart. "Oh, that's great! Thank you," she exclaimed.

"What are housewarming gifts?" I whispered to her.

"When people move to a new place, it's customary for their friends to give them gifts they can use in their new home," she told me.

The only home I'd ever moved into was Green Gulch, and, since I was only three and a half at the time, I hardly remembered that move. However, I was sure nobody had bought us gifts then. I wondered if this were some new custom specifically designed for people who moved to places other than Green Gulch.

I sat silently while everyone brought out their presents. They gave us plates, cups, and other gifts I don't remember. I hoped there would be some toys for my new room, but apparently housewarming presents didn't apply to kids. At age ten, the only gift that interested me was a large, orange food processor. It had lots of blades and crushing things that all fit inside a big bowl, and it looked like you could really mash things up in it.

I don't remember much about the move itself. Some of the Green Gulchers helped us load our few pieces of furniture and other possessions into a big van. Then we got into our new red Honda and wound our way up through the misty bends of Route 1 to our new home.

That afternoon, we unpacked, again with the help of several Green Gulch friends. Our new house seemed very big, at least to my eyes, although I now realize it was really quite average. Still, it was a two-bedroom house and all our own. My bedroom was larger than the tiny one I'd had at Green Gulch, and we even had a basement. There were plum trees in the backyard, and my parents told me they'd be full of fruit in the summer.

In a way, I suppose you could say that our living arrangements had improved dramatically. But, while I might have had a bigger bedroom in a nice house, I didn't have any of the things that had been really important to me at Green Gulch. I didn't have the zendo, the communal dining room, the sound of the gongs reverberating through the valley, or the silence. All I had were the role modeling I'd received, the Buddhist stories I'd been told, and the scraps of poetry from the sutras the monks and laypeople had chanted.

I felt as if my whole world had been blown to pieces. Not only had we left other role models behind, but my parents themselves had changed. Although they didn't completely give up their Buddhist beliefs and practices, they began to live a very different life. My father got a job taking telephone orders for a catalog company. My mother taught nursery school. My father began to let his hair grow out, and instead of his priests' robes, he wore clothes like everyone else on our street. My mother dressed up more than she had at Green Gulch, and she no longer wore her rakusu around her neck. If they practiced their daily meditation, I wasn't aware of it. There was no chanting in our house. We still said a traditional Buddhist grace before meals, but we didn't eat in a communal dining room, and we didn't join any other Buddhist organization. It seemed that, for my parents, Buddhism was no longer as important as it had been.

Before I knew it, we had a color television, a VCR, and cable. I was waking up early every Saturday morning to watch cartoons. On weekends and after school, I rode my bike down to the local convenience store. My parents even raised my allowance so that I could buy sodas and candy bars.

The most special thing I'd ever done with my parents while we were living at Green Gulch was to drive to Los Angeles each spring to visit my grandmother and go to Disneyland. We always drove and we always stayed at my grandmother's. It was a way to save money, but I didn't mind. I enjoyed our trips, and, in any case, I didn't know any other way. But after we left Green Gulch, we stayed in hotels and invited Grandma to visit *us*. Once, we even stayed at the Disneyland Hotel.

I was confused. Green Gulch was the world I'd called my own since I was three and a half. The Zen monastery was the only way of life I knew. Deep in my heart, I believed in Buddhist values. I'd wanted someday to learn to meditate. I'd always wondered what it would be like to be a monk. I'd lived my life with the smell of incense and the tranquillity of silence.

While the physical act of leaving Green Gulch was not, in and of itself, a conflict, it made me consciously aware for the first time of the basic conflict between the world I'd been living in and the larger world I'd always thought of as Outside. And the act of leaving was the cause of all the subsequent conflicts I've been trying to resolve ever since.

From being a Buddhist child in a Buddhist world, I'd become a child trying to be a Buddhist in a non-Buddhist world. I was immersed entirely in the great Other of American/Western culture. Presented with the materialism, popular culture, and noise of this world, I was perplexed and conflicted.

Worst of all, I had virtually no parental guidance or community support to fall back on. There was no community anymore, and my parents had changed so much that they couldn't help me either. I suppose to them, this world, which I saw as Other, was normal. It was, after all, the world they'd grown up in. Buddhism may have been the religion and lifestyle they'd embraced, but to them *it* was still Other. The mainstream culture of our new life was their native ground.

So, they settled into their new life and I tried to settle into mine. There was nothing new about my father's being gone all day, but now, when he returned home, he was stressed out and needed to unwind. At Green Gulch, even when he'd come home late from the zendo, he'd seemed relaxed. If you've spent all day meditating, you don't tend to have too much stress.

As it turned out, Sarah, a friend from Green Gulch, moved out of the community shortly after we did, and her mother found a job at the same company as my father. Although I didn't get to see Sarah very often anymore, I knew that my dad worked with her mother. I also knew that "normal" people worked nine-to-five jobs, but everything was happening so fast that I couldn't quite take it all in. I didn't really understand why *we* were living this type of life, and I even began to wonder if *everyone* at Green Gulch was going to start working at the same company. Of course, that was a child's perspective. I now realize that Sarah's parents were probably going through changes similar to those my own parents were experiencing at the time, and that her mother's going to work at the same company as my father was either a simple coincidence or, possibly, the result of his having recommended her. But you can imagine how odd it all must have seemed to me then.

Even though I'd started fourth grade at my new school several months before we left Green Gulch, the two events have always been associated in my mind. Going to the new school was just one part of the larger change, and it wasn't any easier to adapt to than anything else that was happening to me. The kids there didn't accept me—probably because they didn't understand me any better than I understood them. Most of them came from wealthy families, while I was a Buddhist from a Zen commune and monastery. I was totally out of my element, and as a result I was teased and picked on a lot.

As an indication of just how "foreign" I was, I remember taking a quiz about a story we'd just read concerning a Catholic boy living in a predominantly Protestant neighborhood. One of the fill-in-the-blank questions asked the religion of the central character. Since I thought of religions according to broad categories like Christian, Jewish, Muslim, Hindu, Taoist, Confucianist, or Buddhist, I naturally filled in Christian. The teacher marked me wrong.

The story was obviously written with the assumption that the reader was Protestant, and it was intended to teach a lesson in cultural diversity (as well as to improve our reading skills). It mentioned all the things about this boy that made him different, such as going to catechism and listening to mass in Latin. But the differences between Protestants and Catholics didn't seem very important to me. I was more interested in learning what it was like to go to church and what it meant to be a Christian. It seems ironic to me now that our teacher had tried to get us interested in the things that made being a Catholic "different," but had failed to see that I, as a Buddhist, was "different" on a whole other order of magnitude.

Moving out of Green Gulch made me aware for the first time that I am a religious minority. Just as nonwhites find that white people assume things from a white perspective, women have to deal with hearing everything from a male perspective, and gays get the world taught to them from a straight perspective, I was dished a plate of the religious majority's perspective. We have freedom of religion in America, but this is still a Judeo-Christian country.

Christians and Jews might not think too much about America's being a Judeo-Christian culture, but that's because they're too much a part of the majority to understand the perspective the rest of us have. There have been times when I knew people thought I would be damned to Hell because I didn't believe what they believed. And, on more than one occasion, I've met Christians who've tried to proselytize and convert me to their religion. Others have simply assumed that I believe in concepts like God and Heaven. It sometimes upsets me that people can be so close-minded.

I was never taught that the Buddha thought people who didn't agree with his concept of enlightenment were in any way lost. I believe he respected other philosophies of his time in much the same way that Aristotle respected Plato, even though he disagreed with him. I was brought up to respect other people's beliefs, even though they might be different from mine. All I ask is to be given the same respect in return, and certainly in many instances I am, but there are still many people who, out of ignorance or simple prejudice, seem to consider any nonmonotheistic belief system pagan, and less worthy than their own. In my struggle to come to terms with the many aspects of American culture, this religious bias has been one of the more difficult conflicts for me to resolve.

Today, I hear about people who believe there should be

prayer in public schools and who want Creationism taught instead of Evolution in biology classes. I realize that there are many Christians in America who *don't* believe in either school prayer or teaching Creationism, but as a Buddhist who doesn't pray and doesn't believe the Book of Genesis is anything other than a work of literature, I'm sometimes angered by this kind of prejudice. Sometimes I'm saddened, and sometimes it just scares me.

FINDING THE MIDDLE WAY

In many ways, the longer I lived outside Green Gulch the more I changed, but, from a nondualistic Zen perspective, I wasn't really changing at all. I still had the same Buddhist values I'd always had. I knew about the value of silence and cultivating the meditative mind. And when the kids at my new school teased or tormented me, I tried to be like a samurai: a meditative Zen warrior. I knew that much of popular culture was the stuff of delusion, and that materialism—the desire for money, status, and power—just clouded one's mind and kept one from enlightenment. But, on the other hand, until we left Green Gulch, I'd been deprived of Outside World things. As a result, whenever I was at an "Outside" friend's house, I'd always taken the opportunity to watch as much TV as I could, to finagle a soda, or to get taken to a fast-food restaurant for a burger and fries.

I was a Buddhist, but I was also a kid, and I wanted all the things that were forbidden. All kids do. It's the job of their parents and other adult role models to show them how to be adults, and at Green Gulch, despite the lack of formal Buddhist education, I had learned, through observing the adults' methods, how to be a good Buddhist. I may have had my childish desires, but I also knew the ethics of my religion.

I knew how I was supposed to behave at Green Gulch, but in our new life, I didn't have a clue. As a child, I embraced all the good things I was suddenly offered. But, in many ways I never really adapted to the world outside.

When I physically left Green Gulch and the Zen Center, all I had left of that life were my memories. I recited those memories over and over in my mind until they became a kind of sutra, or text to live by. As I went forward with my life, I clung to that sutra.

The conflicts between my two worlds haven't disappeared; if anything, they've become more pronounced, but whenever a conflict has seemed too difficult to resolve, I've looked back to the old teachings to guide me. I can't say I'm always right, since I'm certainly not enlightened and I, too, have fallen victim to delusion, but I do think that if your belief system is deeply internalized, it will be there to steady you and keep you from falling too hard when you stumble.

THREE

BUDDHIST CULTURE VERSUS POPULAR CULTURE

At Green Gulch, I was taught the Second Noble Truth of the Buddha: Suffering is caused by desire. But avoiding desire, I also learned, does not mean giving up everything you have. Rather it means being content with what you have but not *clinging* to those things or trying to prevent them from leaving you.

Before the Buddha became enlightened, he practiced with a group of ascetics, some of whose beliefs were similar to those he eventually stated as the Four Noble Truths, but who also believed that avoiding desire meant having to give up everything. The Buddha gave up so much that he virtually stopped eating and almost starved to death. Once he became enlightened, however, he realized that ridding oneself of desire was really a question of achieving a balance between becoming too attached to things and denying oneself everything. That balance is achieved by sitting with what you have and waiting to see if it stays with you or if you lose it. If it stays, you truly have it and should cherish it. If it goes, you never really had it. At least, that's what we believe in Buddhism.

As I've already said, I was taught at Green Gulch to avoid popular culture. The adults in the community looked upon popular culture as a form of attachment, and they looked upon people in America as slaves to popular trends. They considered things like popular music, popular fashion, television, and popular movies superficial forms of escapism that fill one's head with delusion and cause one to lose track of what's truly important.

At this point, however, I ought to point out that not everything at Green Gulch was purely black and white. It's true that the Green Gulch culture was very much opposed to popular culture, but our parents weren't so strict that they kept us from having any contact with it at all. We were, after all, children, and our parents sometimes took us to the movies or for ice cream simply because they knew we liked those things.

Also, we weren't as isolated as, for example, the Amish. We attended public school and some of us had friends outside Green Gulch. At school, or when I was with my non–Green Gulch friends, I often heard about such things as superheroes and cartoons. But there were also many things I *didn't* know about popular culture. There were cartoons I'd heard about but never watched and superheroes whose names I knew, but not their powers. So, although I was raised with very strong ideals, the reality of my life didn't always conform perfectly to that ideology.

Going to nursery school on Halloween, age five. I'm dressed as Yellow, the "Rainbow Goblin" (see page 61). You'll notice, in the foreground, other kids in store-bought costumes.

As I've grown up, I've had to decide for myself to what extent I agree with the Green Gulch attitude toward popular culture. Certainly, from a Buddhist perspective, it can be argued that becoming attached to trends is problematic. The Buddhist argument would be that if someone becomes interested or involved with something just because it's "in" and snubs anything that's "out," that person becomes a slave to the in/out list prescribed by society. And it also follows from Buddhist philosophy that people should try not to become attached to anything that's superficial because such things are a form of escapism that keeps us from thinking about what is really important in life, such as love, friendship, inner beauty, or simply figuring out what life is all about.

As I've wandered through the American milieu, I've thought a lot about these Buddhist arguments, and I've come up with a lot of questions. What if I'm interested in something that happens to be "in," but that I genuinely like? What if I feel that a piece of popular entertainment is actually a work of art that's enriching my life? Should I avoid it anyway, just because it's popular? What if I go out and see a movie I know is superficial and a form of escapism because I just need to blow off steam, relax, and enjoy a laugh? Is that being attached to popular culture? I can see both points of view, and ever since I left Green Gulch, they've created a conflict inside me.

Sometimes I have trouble relating to Western culture. Living in the American world, I've encountered many people whose values seem to be very different from mine, and who seem to think that their values are to be preferred, or even the *only* values anyone should have.

I came out of Green Gulch with gigantic holes in my knowledge of popular culture. People are often surprised when I admit to not being familiar with a certain celebrity or not understanding a particular reference. They're always saying things like, "What do you mean you don't know who so-and-so is?" One man I work with was astonished that I'd never heard of Ed Sullivan, and I got the distinct impression that he thought less of me *because* I didn't know who he was.

But I wasn't raised to think that knowing names like his was all that important. And because Green Gulch was more or less isolated, I didn't absorb this kind of information subliminally, as one would living "on the Outside." If I happened to ask about someone I'd heard about, my parents and the other adults at Green Gulch were likely to ask, "Why do you care who that person is?" When I found out that Ed Sullivan had been the host of an extremely popular television variety show, I realized that questions very like theirs were forming in my own mind. Why should I know who Ed Sullivan was? Would knowing about him really help me in my life? Of course, there's nothing wrong with knowing facts about popular culture. Most people who grew up in mainstream America *do* know these facts, but I would hope they don't think any less of someone like me who doesn't always know them.

Sometimes people even seem to pity my lack of knowledge, which leads me to believe they must think it's really important to know such facts. The heads of my friends and acquaintances are filled with popular facts: the names of members in a band whose latest CD went platinum, which actress won the Oscar, and so on.

My questions about the American perspective are several: Why is popular culture so important to American society? Why is following trends so important? Why are some people so surprised that I don't know about some particular element of pop culture? Maybe the man at work was just surprised that I didn't know about something with which he was so familiar. Maybe he didn't even like Ed Sullivan. Not everybody in America likes everything that's popular. But, for any given personality, song, movie, or television program that *is* popular, there must be a critical mass of people who *do* like it, and it really feels to me that those people put tremendous social pressure on the rest of us to like it, too. Otherwise, why would people care so much about what I do or don't know?

My upbringing has taught me that, in the grand scheme of

things, it doesn't really matter whether or not I know about celebrities like Ed Sullivan because my knowledge of him can't bring me true happiness. In fact, I was taught that the popular media actually work to prevent us from achieving enlightenment because they encourage us to rely on the superficial for our happiness rather than finding enrichment in things that are truly important.

TV, TOYS, AND COMIC BOOKS

At Green Gulch, as I've said, I rarely watched television. My parents had a nine-inch, black-and-white TV that they kept in a closet most of the time. Occasionally, they'd let me watch an educational show like *The Electric Company* or *Sesame Street,* but they discouraged me from sitting in front of it on a daily basis, and I learned to entertain myself in other ways. At night, my parents read me stories. I used to go to the public library in Mill Valley and check out records that told stories about King Arthur and Robin Hood.

I also like to invent my own stories. When I played with my friends, we'd make up scenarios rather than rely on story lines inspired by cartoons. When I played with toys, I also made up my own scenarios.

I remember being at a birthday party for one of my few friends who lived outside Green Gulch. I walked past a table full of cupcakes and stacks of napkins with characters from a TV show called *Star Trek.* One of the kids was talking about a program called *Scooby-Doo,* and another mentioned *The Dukes of Hazzard* and *Gilligan's Island.* I'd heard about these shows from the kids at school and friends like the birthday boy who lived outside the community, but I didn't know which of them were live-action and which were cartoons.

Later in the party, the kids were talking about the characters from *Star Trek* that were depicted on the napkins. When I admitted that I'd never watched *Star Trek,* the mother of the birthday boy helped me to learn the characters' names. I remember having trouble distinguishing between Scotty and Mr. Spock because I thought Mr. Spock's name was Mr. Scott.

I didn't read comic books, either. I didn't know much about superheroes or cartoon characters. I didn't play with action figures. Instead, I enjoyed dressing up and playing characters from the stories I liked, which were different from those popularized by cartoons and action figures. My base of knowledge was simply different from that of other children my age.

I had store-bought toys, but my parents tried to buy me ones that didn't rely on cartoons to advertise them. I had a set of toy knights, a castle, and stuffed animals. My favorite stuffed animal was a dragon. In addition to these, however, I also had pieces of cloth and unusual clothes that I used to make costumes for the characters I liked to play.

One day, while I was living at Green Gulch, I was standing around with a bunch of kids at recess. The topic of conversation that day was which superhero we liked best. As we leaned against the wire-mesh fence, each kid gave the name of his favorite superhero. I didn't know many, but I'd heard about some of them. My parents had taken me into town to see *Superman* a few years earlier, and *The Electric Company* had a Spider-Man character. Beyond those, however, I knew only

Batman, the Incredible Hulk, and Wonder Woman, because I'd heard the kids at school talking about them.

I paced along the cracking white and yellow lines that crisscrossed the cement of the playground. I was anxious. I wanted to impress these guys. I didn't want them to think I was stupid or not worth playing with. Although I'd learned to entertain myself in different ways at home, I still felt that I needed to know about superheroes in order to fit in. One by one, all the names I knew, except for Wonder Woman, were used. I didn't want to name Wonder Woman because I thought the other boys would laugh at me for choosing a female character. But I also didn't want to repeat one that had already been mentioned, because then they'd call me a copycat.

The last superhero mentioned was Captain America. It was my turn. I was still scared that if they found out I didn't know anything about superheroes, they wouldn't want to be friends with me. Then, suddenly, I swelled with pride as I thought that maybe I didn't have to know anything about superheroes to get them to like me. I decided at that moment to *make up* a superhero. I thought about what kind of name a superhero should have. Maybe he should have "Captain" before his name. I thought about what superheroes did. Superman could fly. That was the most impressive power I could think of. "My favorite superhero is Captain Flyer," I said.

The other kids were surprised. They'd never heard of Captain Flyer. They asked me what his powers were and how he got them. Over the days and weeks that followed, I told them stories about Captain Flyer. One day, a boy's mother called my mother. She said her son wanted to know when the Captain Flyer program came on. My schoolmates were tricked for a long time. I think they eventually found out I was making it up, but by then they weren't really angry. In fact, they respected me for having been so imaginative and convincing.

On another occasion, I saw some of the boys in my class playing with the action figure of a bare-chested warrior who rode on top of a giant tiger. I asked if I could play. To me, the warrior was Gongar of the Tiger Clan, a fierce barbarian I'd invented on the spot.

"Duh," the other boys sneered. "He's He-Man!" I hadn't watched the *He-Man* TV show. They thought I was really stupid, but I eventually persuaded them to explain it to me. When they finally told me who He-Man was, I thought the concept boring. And, even then, I didn't think a TV show should dictate the ideas we used in our play.

I don't think I was the only one who thought that way. There was, for example, a girl named Anna living at Green Gulch who, one day, came to school with a lunch box covered in multicolored paint. Everyone at school asked her what had been on her lunch box, but she wouldn't say. She'd obviously had a lunch box with popular figures depicted on it but had painted over them. I think Anna was embarrassed by them and preferred the pretty colors she'd put on herself.

Every Sunday at Green Gulch we had a special service for laypeople who lived off campus and anyone else who wanted to come and learn more about Buddhism. It was like a Sunday church service, except that it involved meditation and Zen Buddhist chanting. It was followed by a luncheon and tea.

There were many laypeople who were interested in Buddhism but who lived outside the community as nuclear families in residential neighborhoods. Many of them had children whom they brought to the service. Most were regulars, and their children would accompany them every Sunday.

When they came, I played with these children, who'd had more exposure to popular culture than the Green Gulch kids. One day, some of the children invited me to play a game called TV tag. It worked just like regular tag except that the players would be safe from whomever was "it" so long as they touched the ground and said the name of a television show that hadn't already been named.

We played on the Upper Deck of the Wheelwright Center, in front of the library and just above the dining room. A hill rose up to the height of the second story, and the Upper Deck was built so that you could get onto it from the laundry room, which was built near the top of the hill. The ground on the other side also rose to meet the deck, and a little stone path zigzagged down to the dining room. A boy named Kelly was "it." As he ran at me, I dashed toward the laundry room. I could smell the lint and steam from the shed where the residents washed their clothes. I squatted down and said *"Sesame Street."* As the game continued, it wasn't long before I'd named all the shows I'd ever watched, as well as those I'd only heard about. A boy named Ethan cornered me where the stone path ran down to the dining room. I couldn't think of anything, so he tagged me.

At first, as I chased the other kids, I thought they'd run out of shows to name, as I had. Kelly hit the ground and named a show I'd never heard of. I ran after Ethan, but he stooped down and shouted another name. Apparently there was no end of cartoon characters and there were limitless superheroes. Then there were comedies, action shows, and so forth. I realized that it would be virtually impossible for me to catch anyone.

As I grew up, I began to see more TV. As I've indicated, I was a kid, and I didn't really understand why my parents didn't want me to become involved with popular culture. I was jealous of the kids outside our community who could watch as much as they wanted, and I used to love visiting my grandmother because she had a color television.

Whenever I was at a friend's house outside Green Gulch, I watched as much TV as possible in order to learn about the cartoons everyone was always talking about. Once I almost cried because I had to leave someone's house just as *Scooby-Doo* was coming on. It must have been the first time I saw it, and I got to watch only the opening credits.

At one point, a Green Gulch kid named Sean got a TV with good reception. His mother wouldn't normally have had a set but his parents were divorced and his father, who wasn't a member of the Green Gulch community, had given the TV to Sean as a present. Sometimes, after dinner in the communal dining room, the two of us would sneak off to his house and watch TV in his room. I was probably eight or nine, and it was the first time I'd ever watched TV—other than *Sesame Street* or *The Electric Company*—on a regular basis. I remember watching *The A-Team* every week.

Television, comic books, and cartoons are the aspects of popular culture most available to children, and so my lack of knowledge about them became apparent both to me and to the kids I played with very early in my life. But, as the years went by and I became aware of other aspects of popular culture, I soon realized that I knew no more about them than I did about television, comic books, and cartoons.

MUSIC APPRECIATION

At Green Gulch we sang songs not only during the hours we were in child care but also during special events or on holidays, when the whole community—children, adults, monks, and laypeople—came together.

One night, I remember, we were sitting in the lecture room on the top floor of the Wheelwright Center. The room looked out over a vista of fir trees obscured only by the black paper birds taped to the windows to keep the real birds from flying into the glass. All the monks, priests, laypeople, and children sat around on old, beat-up sofas, donated easy chairs, zafus, and zabatons. As a child of about six, I sang along with some fifty or so children and adults, "You Can't Get to Heaven." In case you're not familiar with the song, the lyrics are somewhat improvisational. They go, "Oh, you can't get to Heaven on a _____, 'cause _____" The singers fill in the blanks with something you can't get to Heaven on and the reason why, as in, "You can't get to Heaven on roller skates 'cause you'll roll right past the pearly gates." Each improvisational verse is followed by the chorus, "I ain't going to grieve, my Lord, no more."

It was an ironic choice in the Zen setting. All the adults understood the song as an old spiritual they'd probably learned in their youth. But we children didn't understand the meaning behind it. I'd heard of something called "Heaven," but I knew it wasn't something we believed in. The Buddha had been reincarnated many times, legend said, so he clearly hadn't gone to Heaven. I wasn't even sure what "my Lord" referred to. I was reading King Arthur and Robin Hood stories at the time, and I knew that lords often figured in medieval folklore, so I actually liked the song because I thought it had to do with medieval times.

I also liked the fact that it was improvisational. As I listened to one person after another make up a lyric, I wanted to make up a verse of my own. I didn't know exactly what I was going to say, but I wanted to be creative so badly that I called out, "I've got one." Everyone looked at me and fell silent, waiting for me to start. "Oh, you can't get to Heaven . . . ," I sang.

"Oh, you can't get to Heaven . . . ," they echoed.

I suddenly realized I didn't have anything in mind to fill in the blanks. I looked around and saw a zafu on the floor. ". . . On a za-a-fu," I sang. Every adult in the room started to laugh.

In child care we sang more popular songs. For example, I remember singing, "Hey, good lookin', whatcha got cookin', how's about cookin' somethin' up with me. . . ." But, generally speaking, my experience with music was oriented toward singing songs rather than listening to them on records or tapes.

One day Sean and another Green Gulch kid named Micah, both of whom were about a year older than I, met me in front of my house to walk to child care, which, that day, was being held in the fields. (We sometimes had child care on our organic farm so that we could learn about farming.) Sean was carrying a magazine he'd gotten from his father that had a picture of a famous singer named Michael Jackson.

All the way down the dirt road to the fields, Sean and Micah told me about Michael Jackson. They'd heard his songs when they were at the home of an off-campus friend, and as we walked they taught me the lyrics to "Beat It."

When we got there, the person in charge heard us talking. As we potted plants in the greenhouse, she joined in our conversation. At one point she mentioned that Michael Jackson was black. "He's not black," I said, innocently. "He's white."

"Na-uh!" Micah and Sean responded together. "Everybody knows Michael Jackson's black."

"Uh-huh," I said, grabbing Sean's magazine and pointing to the picture. "Look at the color of his skin. He's white."

One day, Noah and his twin brother, Aron, also Green Gulch friends, came back from town with a Michael Jackson tape they'd bought and invited me into their trailer to listen to it. I sat on a futon in one of the little trailer rooms while they plugged in a small tape player their parents had in the closet. They pressed Play. Even though I'd already learned the lyrics from Sean and Micah, this was the first time I'd actually heard "Beat It" sung by Michael Jackson himself.

Slowly and gradually, I learned about popular music. Children who are more exposed to Western culture would probably have learned about such things at an earlier age, listening to their older siblings' record collections or listening to albums with their friends. At Green Gulch, however, we didn't have regular access to stereos or albums of popular music, and, in any case, we wouldn't have been allowed to play loud music, even if we had it. Popular music like that of Michael Jackson was something we imported into our world.

• • •

After I moved away from Green Gulch, the kids at my school, who had started listening to the popular bands, would ask me what my favorite group was. When I told them I didn't have a favorite, they laughed. At the time, their teasing hurt. I felt I couldn't be myself when I was with them, and that made me angry. But I also remained proud of being Buddhist.

To this day, I've never really developed an interest in popular music. I've still never been to a rock concert. I don't pay much attention to which groups are popular. If you told me the name of any given singer, half the time I wouldn't recognize it. If I hear a song on the radio, most of the time I don't know who wrote it or who's singing it.

I don't have anything against the kinds of music these kids liked. I don't have anything against people who like to go to rock concerts. But I *did* resent the fact that I wasn't accepted just because the things that interested me weren't popular. Today, I still meet many people who seem to think that liking what's popular is the only way to go. I do listen to music, but I don't listen to anything just because it's popular.

When I listen to music, it's rarely loud. I listen to it loud enough so that I can hear it, but I don't blast it just for the thrill. Sometimes, I just live for a while in silence.

From time to time, I've tried listening to loud music, just to see what it's like. Sometimes I've felt pressure from the people around me to become more interested or to learn more about pop music. And I admit that, although it's foreign to me, a part of me has always been fascinated by its allure. Perhaps that's because it was initially something forbidden.

• • •

Part of me is a good Buddhist and another part doesn't always do good Buddhist things. Part of me is content without popular music because, as a Buddhist, I'd like to think I don't need it in my life. However, as a child, part of me always wanted to experience what I'd never experienced. That part of me wanted to have things like Michael Jackson tapes as soon as they came out and to know who all the hot stars were. That part of me still wonders what a rock concert is like. For a long time, those two parts of me have been in conflict.

When I started high school, it was hard to be a good Buddhist. I wanted badly to fit in, so I went overboard trying to learn all the "cool" bands. For the entire summer before high school, I watched MTV, learning all the names. I spent my whole freshman year buying albums whose videos I'd seen on MTV and whatever the other kids were listening to. I didn't really like the music, but I'd been teased so much in the private school I attended from fourth through eighth grades for not being familiar with popular culture that I really wanted to be accepted. Eventually, however, I realized that what I was doing was delusive. I was becoming attached to trends and following them just to be popular. Now I think I'd have been better off just being myself. Maybe I wouldn't have been considered cool, but if people liked me and wanted to be friends with me anyway, at least I'd have known they were real friends.

When it comes to "music appreciation," I've gone through several phases. In high school, I experimented with listening to heavy metal (but I didn't listen to it loud). In college I liked New Age. Sometimes I like to listen to classical music. Sometimes I listen to jazz on the radio.

Sometimes my neighbors blast their music and I have to play mine very loud just to be able to hear it. I also know that if I lose track of which bands are big, some people will think I'm really weird. For example, I've noticed that it's good to at least know who Christina Aguilera is, even if I don't know any of her songs. That way I don't embarrass myself by saying, "Christina who?" I'd like it better if I *didn't* have to know who someone like that is, because it makes me feel as if I have to follow trends simply to be accepted. But I also understand that if I'm going to live in the world of America, I have to accept some of its rules. I just try to live with a chaotic sort of balance.

FASHION DOS AND DON'TS

It's the same way with fashion. At Green Gulch we had nothing one could really call fashion. In fact, we believed that fashion was superficial, that it was an artifice used by people to disguise their true selves, and that by doing so, they lost some of their humanity.

I think this artifice we call fashion is best defined by that non-Buddhist sage Dr. Seuss in his story "The Sneetches." The Sneetches were sold a star-putter-onner machine, which they used to put stars on their bellies. Some Sneetches put on stars and others did not. The plain-bellied Sneetches were ridiculed by the star-bellied Sneetches until they, too, went through the star-putter-onner machine. However, by that time the star-bellied Sneetches were tired of their stars and wanted to distinguish themselves from the plain-bellied Sneetches. So they got a star-taker-offer machine and removed the stars from their bellies. Now, being plain-bellied was in vogue and the star-bellied Sneetches were ridiculed again for looking gaudy.

I'm not a fashion expert—far from it—but I've observed fashion from the perspective of an outsider. Fashion, as I've observed it, allows people to fit in with society and also provides for a departure from the social norm to a place that becomes the new norm, until the pendulum swings back the other way. In other words, fashion is about moving with society.

At Green Gulch, we wore whatever clothes we had. There was a shed we called the Good Will, although it was not in any way affiliated with the organization of the same name (just a bit of Buddhist humor). Whenever people had something they didn't want anymore, they put it in the Good Will. Clothes of all sizes were hung there on coat hangers, and whenever someone wanted new clothes, he or she could go to the Good Will, find clothes that fit, and simply take them.

My parents also liked to shop at thrift stores, so my wardrobe consisted of whatever clothes they had bought me, clothes that parents of older kids had handed down, and clothes we had found in the Good Will. The same was true for the other children who lived at Green Gulch.

Looking through old photos, I'm amazed how practically we dressed. I wore things like T-shirts whose faded designs were not representative of my own likes or dislikes. It rained a lot at Green Gulch and there were many dirt roads, so there were often mud puddles everywhere. In the old photos, I see that I often wore jeans, because they stood up in the rain. On my feet were rubber boots—not fashionable, but they did the job.

When my family left Green Gulch, I was, to some degree, spared the initial shock of fashion in the outside world because at the school I attended, we wore uniforms. But the uniform code wasn't so strict that fashion didn't creep in.

One day, in history class, our teacher asked us what we thought would be the most useful things to send to poverty-stricken people in Africa. She started listing our suggestions: nonperishable food items, clothing, and so on. One kid thought we should send "Gotcha" shirts so that the Africans would look "cool." I was the only person in the class who didn't know what a Gotcha shirt was.

During middle school—sixth through eighth grades—we started having parties. The other kids wore shirts and pants in bright colors with crazy patterns. Fluorescents were popular, and it wasn't considered unfashionable at the time (the mid-eighties) for men to wear pink—so long as it was fluorescent pink.

I tried to blend in. When I entered the school in fourth grade, I wasn't interested in fashion, but as peer pressure mounted I really wanted to be accepted. I was still a kid, and I saw things in concrete terms. I'd internalized many of the Buddhist beliefs with which I'd been brought up, but I don't think I was able, at that time, to make the association between abstract principles and practical applications. All I was really conscious of was that things had been one way at Green Gulch, and at my new school things were different. A part of me was proud of being Buddhist, but another part of me thought that if I fit in, I'd make friends.

So, I went out and bought the kinds of clothes the other kids were wearing—patterned fluorescent button-up shirts and patterned pants. Then I went to a party in my new clothes. But, apparently, I still hadn't gotten it right. I was told that I shouldn't wear patterned pants with a patterned shirt. I was supposed to wear a patterned shirt with plain pants or patterned pants with a plain shirt. Once more, I was confused and upset because I just didn't understand the rules. No one at Green Gulch had taught me the rules of this game.

When I started high school in 1988, I was still somewhat shell-shocked from my K–8 experience. I was beginning to feel that I'd never fit in, and I still hadn't done enough soul-searching to stand on the principles of my Buddhist background. My top priority was still to make friends and be accepted. I decided to go all-fashion. I asked my parents to buy me a leather jacket, but they said it was too expensive, and, anyway, I didn't need a leather jacket to make me happy. That was a very Buddhist response, but it was also confusing, because, although my parents still considered themselves Buddhists, they'd turned their backs on Green Gulch and more or less returned to the culture they'd grown up with. Nevertheless, I wore jeans and a denim jacket as an alternative to the leather jacket, and I slicked back my hair with gel.

I thought I looked cool, but I wasn't sure what the "right" look was. I only knew what I'd seen on TV, and this seemed like something that would blend in. On the first day of art class, my teacher told me I had a "fifties" look. I was annoyed because I'd thought I was contemporary.

As it turned out, the students at my high school were much more relaxed about fashion than those in my previous school had been. They wore less flamboyant, comfortable clothing like khaki pants and T-shirts. (Ironically, my high school had been founded in the 1960s by hippies who wanted their children to attend a school that would nurture their individuality, and its values were in many ways anti–popular culture.) A few of the girls seemed to think my look was sexy, and that was a plus, but in general I started to realize that I *still* didn't really fit in because I'd given up on being myself.

First, I'd been rejected for not fitting in. Then, when I tried to fit in, I stood out for trying too hard. Gradually, I began to dress more "normally," adopting what I thought of as a more or less fashionless style. But then, the nineties arrived and, within the space of a year, Western fashion once more changed radically and abruptly. During my freshman year at Reed College (in 1992) I saw grunge for the first time. I saw body piercings, shaved heads, and purple hair. Once more, I didn't fit in.

Since I'd spent the seventies at Green Gulch, I had no concept of the fact that what was popular in the eighties was any different from what had been popular in the seventies. I'd always looked at the world in terms of Green Gulch on the one hand and everything else on the other. I thought that once I'd figured out how to adapt to American fashion, that would be it. I didn't realize fashion would change.

If you followed the Dr. Seuss story, you'll have realized that there are really two types of Sneetches, regardless of the status of their bellies. The first group is in fashion throughout the story and the second group is always out of fashion. For me, the issue wasn't star-bellied versus plain-bellied Sneetches but rather the understanding that I was always in the second category, on the wrong side of the pendulum.

• • •

It has always baffled me how much attention people in the modern Western world devote to being on the right side of the fashion pendulum. Fashion has always seemed superficial to me. I guess I've just never understood it. I can understand wanting to look good, but I can't understand why it should be so important to look like everyone else. The thing I have the most trouble understanding is why fashion changes and why it's so bad to wear something that just recently went out of fashion. Obviously, I spent a lot of time growing up trying to get the hang of it, but that was really more about trying to be accepted in my new world than it was about being interested in fashion, and, as you'll have seen, it never really worked for me.

I don't think there's necessarily anything either pro- or anti-Buddhist about looking or dressing any particular way. In fact, I think a good Buddhist should be accepting of people no matter how they look. But, to me, one's "look" is not necessarily the same as what I define as "fashion." To me, fashion means adhering to the look that's currently "in." I don't think there's anything wrong with dressing well. For me, the problem begins when "looks" get tied to "trends." I believe that fashion, as I've defined it, is often used as a disguise to make people appear to be something they're not, and, therefore, to keep them from being everything they can be as individual human souls.

My struggles with fashion have taught me two lessons: that, in the long run, I'll probably make better quality friends just being myself than I will by trying to fit in, and that, even though fashion goes in cycles, I can still be myself. Today, I just dress to please myself. If people think I look funny or out of fashion, that's their problem. If people accept me, even though I might not be in the height of fashion, then those are the people I want to be my friends.

HOLIDAY CHEER

Most people don't seem to associate holidays with popular culture. We think of holidays as being religious, like Christmas and Easter; national, like the Fourth of July; cultural, like Saint Patrick's Day; or simply traditional, like New Year's Eve. But all these holidays are also part of our popular culture. If you walk into almost any store just before a major holiday, you'll see symbols of that holiday strung up all over the place. Holiday seasons are integral to our consumer marketing strategies.

At Green Gulch we celebrated some holidays traditionally, we had our own variations on others, some we observed completely differently, and, of course, we also had our own Buddhist holidays.

At Christmas, we followed some of the same customs and traditions as people Outside, but there were also subtle differences. Like everyone else, we gathered together, decorated a tree, did Christmas arts and crafts, and had a Kriss Kringle exchange. One of my fondest memories is of making a gingerbread house with the other Green Gulch kids. And, as a child, I always enjoyed singing Christmas carols. They were good songs. But we didn't believe in the divinity of Christ.

I think, to a large degree, the concept of Santa Claus helped. We didn't need Jesus to have Christmas cheer. To us, Christmas cheer meant being kind to one another, and Jesus wasn't the only religious figure to preach kindness to others. In

Buddhism, we believe in having compassion for everyone. We all suffer in our lives, but that's all the more reason to come together and give. If desire is the root of all suffering, maybe giving is the root of bliss.

The main difference between our ways of celebrating and those of America in general was really a matter of scale. Every year around Christmastime, I seem to read an article in the paper that talks about families going into debt by charging massive amounts of money on their credit cards to buy their children videogame systems, new computers, and whatever else they may have asked Santa Claus to bring them.

Department stores and malls often feature lavish Christmas decorations and sometimes even choruses singing Christmas carols. There is invariably a place where children can sit on Santa's lap and tell him what they want for Christmas. The decorations, the chorus, and Santa are very much a part of the American Christmas tradition, but they are also an invitation to spend more than one can really afford, and they cater to an extremely materialistic interpretation of what is meant by "holiday spirit."

At Green Gulch we were not so materialistic. Our parents never took us to the mall to sit on Santa's lap and they never ran up extravagant credit card bills. Although we exchanged presents, and our parents tried to please us, they bought us only what they could afford. And since we were discouraged from becoming involved with popular culture, we didn't feel the pressure to have the hottest, newest, and invariably the most expensive toy just because "all the other kids" would be getting it. Our parents also taught us to be content with what we had, so we always appreciated the toys we *did* receive.

I'm sure you all know the Christmas carol about the little drummer boy, who was too poor to give Jesus a present and played his drum instead. While I'll discuss our Buddhist attitude toward materialism in the following chapter, let me just say here that at Green Gulch we believed there was a danger in being seduced by the materialism of Christmas. I was raised to believe that it's Buddhist to give to others, but it's un-Buddhist to give more than one can afford, and that the most priceless gifts, like love, don't cost anything at all.

I still believe that. I think Christmas should be about giving and spreading good cheer, not about desire. I think gift-giving can be a very Buddhist act, but only if it is not equated with materialism. To me, the little drummer boy is not only a good Christian. Although he may never have meditated or read a Buddhist sutra, I think he's a good Buddhist as well.

We celebrated Halloween in fairly traditional fashion, dressing up in costumes and going trick-or-treating. However, trick-or-treating was much safer at Green Gulch than in some other neighborhoods. We went from shack to trailer asking for candy and then hit the gaitan (where the monks stayed). Because we knew everyone and everyone was a member of the congregation, we never had to worry about people doing nasty things to the candy, and we were never concerned about being sprayed with shaving cream or harassed by teenagers.

We Green Gulch children were always creative at Halloween. One year, a couple of girls who were several years older than I dressed up as "noncolors." One painted her face all black and the other painted hers all white.

Without TV or movies, one of my main sources of fiction

came from the bedtime stories my mother read to me. One of these was called *The Rainbow Goblins*. There were seven goblins, each of whom was named after one of the colors of the rainbow. Each one carried a bucketful of the essence of his color. Their leader was Yellow. One October, I decided to be Yellow for Halloween.

I showed up at my nursery school in Sausalito on Halloween day in a goblin costume my mother had sewn for me. I had gray skin, a blue vest with a pointy collar, and pointy ears. I carried a bucket lined with yellow plastic. As I left my mom's car and entered the stream of children marching into the nursery school, I saw that most of the others wore costumes their parents had bought.

Even though the communal dining room at Green Gulch provided food for everyone, my mother bought groceries on a regular basis so that we'd have food for breakfast, which we didn't usually eat in the dining room, and for my school lunches. One day, while I was in the supermarket with her, I'd seen racks of prefabricated costumes, each consisting of a plastic mask, a plastic shirt, and plastic pants. Whether it was a devil costume or a Superman costume, it had the same plastic components. The only difference was in the way they were painted. That day at school, there were several dozen plastic witches, ghosts, vampires, Frankensteins, mummies, devils, at least two C-3POs from *Star Wars*, and no less than four identical Spider-Men. The kids thought my Yellow costume was weird, because they didn't know the story, but I was proud of it. I thought I had the best costume of all. (Perhaps this was the beginning of my ongoing battle to master the mysteries of fashion!)

• • •

By far the most dramatically "different" holiday for us was New Year's Eve. We would all eat a special dinner in the dining room. Then, after dinner, various members of the community would perform. Their "acts" could be anything from comedy to magic tricks to playing a musical instrument.

After the performances, a few of the laypeople wheeled in a movie projector while several others erected a screen, and we all watched cartoons followed by a main feature. It was on a New Year's Eve, for example, that I first saw *20,000 Leagues Under the Sea*. After the movie, the children were put to bed. Then the adults, both laypeople and monks, went to the zendo to meditate until midnight.

Sometimes time seems to pass very quickly, and there's nothing we can do about it. Buddhism teaches that things always change, and time is no exception. One key concept in Buddhism is the Eightfold Path. The Buddha taught that in order to pursue enlightenment, it is not enough just to think deeply or just to meditate for a long time. In fact, he said that there is no one thing you can do that will make you enlightened; rather there are eight things you have to practice all at the same time. These are right view, right intention, right speech, right action, right livelihood, right effort, right mindfulness, and right meditation. He called the path to enlightenment that follows these eight things the Eightfold Path. In keeping with the concept of right mindfulness, I've always thought that it's important to be *mindful* of the passage of the years. New Year's Eve, for me, is a time to celebrate, but it's also a time to be reflective and contemplative. Even as a child, I knew that a good deal of the fun the adults provided on New

Year's Eve was for the benefit of us children. I also knew that the adults meditated afterward, and I came to understand that being meditative on New Year's Eve was a part of reaching maturity.

In Western culture, New Year's Eve sometimes seems more like a festival of Dionysus than a commemoration of the passage of time. It's traditional to drink champagne, to go to parties, to be loud, and to cheer when the clock strikes twelve. But I wonder how many Westerners see the sun rise on New Year's Day (unless they haven't been to bed yet) or even wake up before noon.

I have nothing against celebrations or pleasure, but for me, mindfulness shouldn't take a backseat to entertainment and intoxication when commemorating the passage of time. For a long time, I didn't participate in a traditional New Year's celebration. It was often hard when everyone else was partying and I wasn't, but I usually tried to meditate at night, get up on New Year's morning to watch the sunrise, and then have a big breakfast.

On December 31, 1999, I had my one and only Western-style New Year's experience. I decided that I would regret not knowing what everyone else was experiencing on that millennial occasion. I had also been curious all my life as to what it was like. So I went into downtown San Francisco, had a good deal to drink (for me, anyway), and stood with almost a quarter of a million people in the Embarcadero watching the festivities.

The next morning, I had my first hangover (getting drunk isn't encouraged in Buddhism, either—in fact, you may remember that one of the sixteen vows taken by Buddhist monks is not to become intoxicated). I got up with great effort and watched the sunrise from my deck. Then I went back to sleep and was in something of a haze all morning. I'd wanted to spend the first day of the year 2000 thinking about the twenty-first century, but, hungover as I was, and hurt by the rising sun, I thought and felt nothing. I'm glad I had the experience. It was enlightening in and of itself because I participated as an observer. But it also restricted the enlightenment I could have gained otherwise.

One holiday that's unique to my background is Buddha's Birthday, which comes around Easter time. We children were almost never allowed to participate fully in religious practices at Green Gulch. We didn't meditate or chant. We had to learn about our religious heritage primarily through observing the adults and asking questions. But Buddha's Birthday was an exception. It was a day for the kids.

The person in charge of child care would read the legend of the Buddha to us. When an Indian prince named Siddhartha Gautama was born, the story goes, it was prophesied that he would become a great sage. The prince's father, the king, didn't want him to become a sage, so he forbade his son to leave the palace in the hope that he wouldn't contemplate the woes of the world.

One day the prince left the palace anyway and saw the suffering that was outside. He saw a sick man, an old man, and a dying man. He decided to find the root of this suffering and learn how to eliminate it from the world, so he joined a group of ascetics. The ascetics thought that denying the body was the key to avoiding suffering, so they went with almost no food, water, or sleep. Siddhartha was so devout that he ate only one sesame seed a day, drank only one drop of water a day, and slept only one hour a day.

Then one day a woman, who was coming down to the river to offer a bowl of rice to the river god, saw Siddhartha lying on the shore, dying. She gave him the bowl of rice and thus saved his life. Siddhartha realized then that he had been going about it all wrong. The key to avoiding suffering was neither the life of a prince nor the life of an ascetic. He had to find a way in which he didn't deny himself the truth but didn't deny his body either. He called this the Middle Way.

He sat under a tree for forty-nine days. At the end of that time, he realized the Four Noble Truths and came to understand the Eightfold Path. At that moment, Siddhartha was fully enlightened and became the Buddha.

After being read the legend of the Buddha, we children went to the celebration, in which we played important roles. The festivities took place on the grassy square at the center of Green Gulch where an altar had been erected along with a wicker shrine entirely covered with flowers. In this flower shrine was a tray filled with sweet tea. Standing in the pool of tea was a statue of the baby Buddha.

The adults gathered in a circle around the altar and the shrine. The priests came out and conducted a ceremony in front of the altar, ringing bells, lighting incense, and chanting. Then the congregation chanted the Heart Sutra.

After that, we children paraded out. Some of us carried a flower-filled cart in the shape of a six-tusked elephant, which was meant to represent the elephant that had appeared to the Buddha's mother in a dream, proclaiming that her son would be a great sage. Other children paraded in front and in back of the cart throwing additional flower petals. Finally, everyone walked in a slow procession to the shrine to pour sweet tea over the baby Buddha. It was always the privilege of the children to be the first to pour the tea.

After the ceremony, the dragon came out. Some of the adults had built a dragon out of Styrofoam. We would attach kite string to it in four places and tie gigantic helium balloons to the top. The dragon rose from the ground as four or more adults held the kite strings, trying to make the dragon buck around and look as if it were really flying.

This holiday is still very important to me. It's essentially the only Buddhist holiday I participated in as a child and it's part of my identity. Over the years it's changed. For example, when I went back to Green Gulch in 1993, they were serving birthday cake in an attempt to make the celebration more "Western." I understand their reasoning. They wanted to claim Buddhism as American, but most of those people were converts, not second-generation Buddhists.

FINDING THE MIDDLE WAY

Some other boy, growing up in a Buddhist country such as Thailand, Burma, or Tibet, would have been raised entirely in the culture of that country, but, as a result of my upbringing, I've been exposed to two cultures and am caught, in effect, between two worlds. The truth is that I don't always know exactly where I stand in the labyrinth that snakes its way between Buddhist culture and American popular culture.

I believe in the Buddhist attitude toward popular culture. I think there's a danger in becoming attached to trends, and I think that popular culture prevents us from focusing on the less superficial and more substantive things that are important in our lives. But, living in America, I've also learned that I can't remain ignorant of popular culture. Being a plain-bellied Sneetch doesn't spare me from the popularity game. People will judge me on the way I look even if I don't think about how I look. Like the kids in my middle school, they'll continue to ask me what kind of music I listen to. I can't escape that.

I can't escape from myself, either. The part of me that holds these opinions about popular culture is just one part of me. There's another part that desires popular culture and does sometimes become attached to trends. It would be nice to think I'm some sort of sage, but I'm not. I'm not pure. I like candy, sodas, watching TV, going to movies, and other forms of popular entertainment. Throughout my life, there have been times when I've strayed from the Eightfold Path.

Sometimes I've tried to rebel against popular culture. Sometimes I've tried to fit in. Sometimes I've been like a plain-bellied Sneetch trying to put stars on his belly. Sometimes I've tried to remove the stars when everybody else had them.

The stuff of which our personalities are made consists of polarities, axes, opposites, and multivalent facets. As much as I believe that desire is the root of all suffering, I also believe that all opposites should exist in balance. Where's my balance? How do I live in popular culture and still remain true to Buddhist culture? How do my poles and facets come together, and along what axes? How do I find the Middle Way?

First of all, I don't think that everything in popular culture is necessarily bad. For example, I sometimes go out to the movies on a weekend because I've had a tough week at work and need to blow off steam. I don't think that's superficial, because what I'm really doing is taking some necessary downtime from the hectic world I now live in. There are also TV shows, music, popular fiction, and so forth, that I like. But I think that's okay, too. Sometimes the things I like are totally unpopular and sometimes they happen to be popular. I don't let trends dictate my taste. I know what I like and I stick to that. One of my favorite novels is J.R.R. Tolkien's *The Lord of the Rings*. One of my least favorite novels is Charles Dickens's *Great Expectations*. Movies I've liked include *Sleepy Hollow, Edward Scissorhands,* and *The Godfather*. Movies I've disliked include *Independence Day, The Blair Witch Project,* and *Interview with the Vampire*. In music, I like Bob Dylan, Tangerine Dream, and most classical music, but I dislike most of today's pop music.

But I think I've also, from time to time, gone astray. I went through a phase shortly after college when I really got involved with playing video games because all my friends had Play-Stations or Sega Saturns or computers with powerful graphics and sound cards that allowed them to play the newest, hottest computer games. I followed that trend and soon I, too, had a PlayStation and a powerful computer on which I could play the same computer games. After a while, I was spending almost all my spare time playing video games. Eventually, it got to the point where I wasn't going out much and I wasn't always paying attention to what was going on in the world. My involvement with video games had gone from using them for relaxation to their becoming a form of escapism. As soon as I realized that, I stopped playing those games. I don't think there's anything wrong with computer or video games per se, but I don't play them anymore because I know how easily I can be seduced by them.

So, although I still believe what Buddhism teaches about popular culture, I've tried to adapt to American culture. I think the people at Green Gulch were in many ways too rigid in rejecting everything about popular culture. Over the years, I've tried to figure out for myself which aspects of it are okay from a Buddhist point of view and which are still problematic for me as a Buddhist.

I also think Green Gulch was too isolated. Of course, the adults there were aware of popular culture because they'd grown up with it, but, as a kid growing up at Green Gulch, I was kept largely ignorant of it. And I believe that even the adults, because of their isolation, were too unaware of the changes that were occurring in the world outside. Anyone who is truly on the path to enlightenment should, I think, remain open to being aware of popular culture. There's a danger, I believe, in Buddhists becoming so isolated that we don't see what's going on around us. (Of course, saying that makes it hard for me to always practice what I preach because there's a lot about which I'm still unaware. I can, however, make a point of becoming more open to the popular world from now on.)

In short, I've come to disagree with some of the values I was raised with at Green Gulch. I still have Buddhist values, but I've decided for myself how to interpret Buddhist philosophy. I'm my own Buddhist.

But even figuring out all these things for myself doesn't resolve all my problems. Sometimes the contradictions still swirl around in my head. When that happens, I sit Zen meditation, clear my mind, and just *be*. I think the best way for me to navigate the labyrinth is just to be who I am. People might not always understand me, but I think people are less likely to misunderstand someone who's open and matter-of-fact than someone who's pretending to be what he isn't.

FOUR

NONMATERIALISM VERSUS MATERIALISM

Green Gulch was not only a Buddhist monastery, it was also an organization run as a commune, so that all members of the group were meant to contribute to the good of the whole. The people who chose to live there did so in order to be able to practice Buddhism diligently for its own sake, not to accrue wealth or power. As a result, nonmaterialist sentiment carried a double whammy for members of the group. Not only does Buddhism teach that accumulating material goods will not make one happy, but the principles of communal living dictate that self-interest be sublimated to what is in the best interest of the community.

THE NONMATERIALISTIC IDEAL

At Green Gulch all members of the community received free room and board and, in addition, a monthly allowance that was equal for all, regardless of the hours they worked. The pay scale was $100 a month for individuals; $200 a month for couples; and $400 a month for families.

Our living quarters were far from luxurious, but they were adequate for our needs, and since I had never known any other way of living, they seemed "normal" to me.

If you walked uphill from the main zendo complex, past the carpentry shed and the welding shed, you came to a gravel parking lot. If you climbed a flight of hand-built steps and crossed a creek by means of a splintery wooden bridge, you came to the base of a hill covered with long, golden grass. We lived at the top of that hill in a house known as the Bullpens.

Our community was built on what had originally been a ranch. The Green Gulch carpentry crew had built our house (and they built it well, since a number of the students had been carpenters before coming to Green Gulch) from what remained of the old bullpens, and the name stuck.

The Bullpens was a small cottage, probably smaller than the average American house. It was long, with two wings—if you could call them that. Each wing had a small porch and a separate door. Down the center of the house was the bathroom, which divided the two tiny wings.

We lived in the left wing; another family lived in the right; and we shared the bathroom, which was actually divided into three small rooms. The first was a small, boxy room with a low ceiling, unpainted, dark brown, wooden walls, and a spider in each corner. It housed the compost toilet that consisted of a wooden cover over a deep pit. Next to the toilet was a box full of sawdust. When you finished using the toilet, you scooped up a trowel-full of sawdust and poured it into the pit to cover the smell. A second little room adjacent to the toilet room housed a sink and some towels.

In the third room was our bathtub. This room was covered in neat tiles and the Japanese-style tub was enormous and made of wood, like a hot tub. When it was filled, I could stand up to my neck in hot water. We never had to worry about using too much water because Green Gulch had its own reservoirs, and I enjoyed many nights immersed in that steaming tub.

Our living room was about the size of a small bedroom—just big enough for a couch, a coffee table, and a wood-burning stove, which was our main source of heat. My parents' bedroom was about as small as a bedroom could be. Next to it was my father's study, which was even smaller. He kept his Buddhist paraphernalia there, including a closet full of priests' robes, a zafu, incense, and a calligraphy set. Sometimes members of the congregation came to consult him there on matters of Buddhist ideology. My own room was about the size of a walk-in closet. Somehow I was able to fit in a low sleeping loft, a chest of drawers, and some cubbyholes for my toys, but it was hardly a room.

We had no dining room, and our kitchen was a small alcove in the living room between my parents' bedroom and mine. It was just big enough for a refrigerator and a sink. There was no stove, so we had to manage with a toaster oven, which was adequate only because we ate most of our meals in the communal dining room.

In fact, the Bullpens was one of the nicer houses at Green Gulch, and we lived there because my father was an important priest. Many families, as I've said, lived in trailers. A few lived in houses even smaller than ours, hardly larger than shacks, with just one main room and a couple of sleeping areas.

The only house that was above any of these standards belonged to the abbot, Richard Baker, known as Baker Roshi, who was Shunryu Suzuki's successor. Baker Roshi's house was surrounded by a wall of bamboo. Through a little gate and beyond the bamboo was a lovely Japanese garden, landscaped with bonsai trees, beautiful rocks, and stone decorations, which was perfectly maintained by his students.

Inside the house were many antique tansus or Japanese bureaus. The walls were lined with elegant fans and hand-painted Japanese scrolls. All over were statues of the Buddha and other Japanese sculptures. Most if not all of the art had been given to the community by wealthy donors. The house itself was very large (at least by Green Gulch standards), with spacious halls, a full-size kitchen, a full dining room, a bathroom, and several large bedrooms. It also had an adjacent meditation room where Baker Roshi could meditate in private.

As a child, I was seldom allowed to enter that house, which was legendary at Green Gulch, and the few times I visited there, I thought being the abbot must have been really wonderful. Now, of course, it seems to me hypocritical that Baker Roshi lived so luxuriously while the rest of us lived so simply, but, as we shall see, Baker Roshi was not necessarily the best or purest proponent of our nonmaterialist way of life.

The dining room was, in many ways, the heart of Green Gulch, and the food we ate there was indicative of the pure and practical lifestyle the community had chosen to lead. The room was lined with rows of tables covered with checkered cloths, and it always smelled of bread, onions, and soy sauce. We children generally ate together at one table rather than with our parents.

At the start of each meal, a priest came before the congregation holding a set of wooden clappers. We would all chant:

We venerate the Three Treasures
And give thanks for this food,
The work of many people,
And the suffering of other forms of life.

The Three Treasures are the Buddha, founder of Buddhism and a perfectly enlightened being; the Dharma, and the Sangha, which, as I've already said, are the Buddha's teachings or path to enlightenment, and the congregation of Buddhists. When we finished our recitation, the priest would bang the clappers together.

The chant was not a prayer, because we don't pray in Buddhism, but it *was* a veneration of the things that were important to us, particularly in the context of eating. A good Buddhist should be thankful for his or her food and for the people who provided and prepared it, because we don't take things for granted. We also try to have compassion for the suffering of other life forms when we eat. We never ate meat in the dining room, but when we did eat it elsewhere from time to time as an individual choice, we were mindful of the suffering of the animals who had provided the meat.

After venerating the Three Treasures, we were free to begin the meal. The food was served buffet style and generally consisted of large bowls of salad, brown rice, vegetable pot pies, tofu, and other vegetarian dishes. There was always a plate of bread and a bowl of fruit. Although our meals were healthful and abundant, they were also rather bland. As a result, we kids tended to fill up on bread and butter, fruit, and other un-cooked foods. Each table was set with salt, pepper, and soy sauce, and I remember an older boy showing me how to put soy sauce on my food to give it more flavor. Possibly as a re-sult, I've hated soy sauce to this day!

Virtually everything served in the dining room was prepared in our own kitchens from produce grown organically and ani-mals raised on our own land. If you walked downhill from the zendo, facing the salty wind that blew up from Muir Beach, you came to a wooden gate that marked the beginning of our six fields, each one divided from the next by a wall of ever-greens. All of the fields were ripe with the aroma of peas, chard, carrots, and other produce. One field contained an enormous herb garden and a greenhouse. We even grew our own tea leaves. There was also a wonderful boysenberry patch, chickens that supplied our eggs, and a cow that pro-vided our milk.

What we ate was, on both a practical and a symbolic level, emblematic of our pure, nonmaterialist style of life. We sel-dom had sweets, except perhaps for cake and ice cream at birthday parties and candy on Halloween, and I almost never had soda. The sweetest liquid I ever drank at Green Gulch was fruit juice. As children, of course, we wanted these things, and I can remember our trying to get our hands on sweets as often as possible. Whenever I visited a friend outside the community, I'd eat all the ice cream, hamburgers, and junk food, and drink all the sodas, I could get.

One of the things that made our annual visit to my grand-mother in southern California so special was the treats my mother always packed for the eight-hour drive. I remember stopping at a rest area and getting a tuna fish sandwich, a Reese's Peanut Butter Cup, and a Schweppes ginger beer—common lunch fare for most people, but rare enough to be memorable for me.

On another memorable occasion, I was in second grade and a bunch of kids convinced me to skip out at recess and go to the corner convenience store for candy. I stared at what seemed to me an endless array of choices, all in colorful wrap-pings with fancy writing on them. I didn't know one from the other, and, in the end, I just grabbed something. When we got to the counter, I realized I didn't have any money. I wasn't used to paying for things, and it just hadn't occurred to me that I'd have to. One of the kids paid for my candy bar, and when we got back to the schoolyard I ate it all at once. It was covered with chocolate and had caramel and nuts inside. To me it was exciting and outrageous, and I don't think the other kids really understood how special it was for me. The boy who'd paid my way said I owed him a quarter. I hadn't thought of that either. I guess I'd just assumed he was treating me, and I don't think I ever paid him back.

I remember many other, similar occasions, such as the first time my mother took me to a doughnut shop and I was so overwhelmed by the variety of choices—glazed, sugar, crumb, raised, cake, old-fashioned—that I wound up choosing plain. But the point is really just to indicate that the residents of

Green Gulch, on the whole, really did try to live according to their Buddhist, nonmaterialistic ideals, and to maintain a pure and simple lifestyle.

I also remember my mother explaining to me, in terms I could understand, the problems with popular, mainstream toys. I had a toy ray gun I really liked. When you pulled the trigger, red lights flashed and a laser sounded. It was exciting, but I lost it. Taking pity on me, my mother generously offered to buy me a new one. She drove me down the long, winding road to town, and when we got to the toy store I saw a Luke Skywalker action figure. I wanted it so badly that I begged her to buy it for me. She told me she might get it for my birthday, but I wanted it there and then. At that point my mother said it was the same price as the laser gun, so I could have one or the other, but not both.

I chose the action figure, probably because all the kids at school had *Star Wars* figures, and as soon as we got home, I opened the package and put the blaster in Luke's hand. Then I realized I couldn't play with it because I didn't have any other *Star Wars* figures. My old ray gun had been more fun. It lit up and made noise. I could pretend I was a space ranger. I could pretend to be any number of characters, including one I'd made up. If I wanted, I could even pretend to be Luke Skywalker.

When I complained to my mother, she explained that she didn't think *Star Wars* figures were worth collecting because, even though each one individually was cheap, you needed a lot of them to be satisfied. So, in reality, collecting *Star Wars* figures was expensive compared to the pleasure one got from them.

Left to right: Sean, Robin, and I sitting on a couch at Green Gulch.

THE NOT-SO-IDEAL REALITY

Everything I've said about the Green Gulch culture and the principles I learned there is true, and it's also true that those principles have formed the basic values upon which I've built my life. In retrospect, however, I've come to understand that there were discrepancies and inconsistencies between what we were taught in principle and what was actually taking place.

Some of those inconsistencies lived within me because, in addition to being a Buddhist, I was also a normal kid. So, while I believed, on the one hand, that desire would lead only to suffering, I was still jealous when Sean (the same kid who had the television) received a very extravagant birthday present from his father, who, as I've said, didn't live at Green Gulch. When I arrived at the trailer he shared with his mother to attend his birthday party, I saw many presents, including two enormous boxes from his father, piled on the floor. When Sean tore the paper off those big boxes, a shower of green army men spilled out of the first. It looked to me as if there were more than a thousand. In the second box were dozens of green plastic tanks, helicopters, Jeeps, and army cannons. I couldn't believe his father had given him so much, and when I got home, I begged my mother to get me the same things. When she explained that Sean's father gave him expensive presents to make up for the love he wasn't always there to give, I said, in typical little-boy fashion, that I wished my father would divorce her so that he could give me extravagant presents, too. With great forbearance, as I now understand it, she told me I'd probably be happier with Dad's love than I would be with his gifts. But when my birthday rolled around, my parents did give me a giant tank and a boxed set of army men that included several dozen soldiers and accessories. Although my gift wasn't nearly as grand as Sean's, I was able to let go of my envy, forget about his toys, and enjoy my own.

There were, however, other, more profound inconsistencies and inequalities that had nothing to do with my own childish conflicts, but that became apparent even to me toward the end of my family's stay at Green Gulch. In fact, on more than one occasion, they involved my own family and my father's position as tanto, or head priest.

One day, when I was playing on the Upper Deck and my mother was sitting at a picnic table outside the lecture hall, she motioned me to come over and told me, in a low voice, as if she was afraid someone might overhear, that Baker Roshi and the Board of Directors were going to buy my father a new car. Up until then, my parents had driven a 1960s Volvo with cracked vinyl seats, but, according to my mother, because of his position as tanto, it had been decided that my father needed a more reliable vehicle to get him to and from the Zen Center in San Francisco.

The three of us went together to the Honda dealership in San Francisco to pick it out. I'd never seen so many new cars in so many colors, and I remember being very excited. Finally, after showing us several new models, the salesman went into another room with my father, and when they came out, we were the owners of a new, bright red Honda Accord. My mother drove the Volvo home and I rode proudly with my father in the Honda.

The gravel parking lot at Green Gulch was lined with VW Bugs, an assortment of other old cars, an orange Econoline van, and a small, blue Datsun. Many Green Gulch residents didn't own cars and would often carpool in the Econoline or the Datsun. I didn't brag about our new car because my parents had told me not to, and, in any case, I didn't think it was very enlightened to brag about my good fortune. Nevertheless, having that car was a tremendous boost to my ego, and I couldn't help beaming with pride for my family.

Another example of the preferential treatment my father received as a result of his position involved our allowance. One night my family had dinner at home rather than in the dining room, and, as we were sitting around our little table in the Bullpens, my parents told me they had some good news. Our allowance was going to be raised to $800 a month, twice as much as the allotment for other families. My parents again warned me not to mention this because other people might be jealous, but the increase made me proud. I didn't know how much allowance Baker Roshi got, but I knew my family was going to be the richest in Green Gulch except for the Bakers.

I understood that my father was an important figure in the community. He officiated at the altar during most of our rituals. Another priest might carry the incense, but he always handed the burning stick to my father to put into the burner. He also led the Buddha's Birthday festivities, and people came to our house or his office in the gaitan for counseling. He gave lectures, and when people bowed to him, they bowed lower than they did to almost everyone else at Green Gulch except Baker Roshi. For those reasons, I naïvely assumed that my father must be more enlightened than everyone else and therefore deserved to be treated better. I believed Baker Roshi had given us a larger allowance because we were a respected family.

When I grew up, I thought, I wouldn't work in the fields or on the carpentry crew but would be a priest like my father. I'd spend all my time in the zendo pursuing enlightenment, and people would look up to me just as they looked up to him. I thought someday I too would receive respect for *my* merit.

Today I realize that the "raise" my father received really was a form of materialism. And I think now that Baker Roshi gave it to him in order to justify his own extravagances. I don't doubt that he gave himself a much bigger "raise" than he gave my father.

When I was seven years old, the Hawken family came to Green Gulch and moved into a trailer right next to the Bullpens. I became friendly with their son, Aidan, who was about my age.

When, one day, my mother again made a special dinner for us to eat at home, I couldn't help suspecting that this signaled another secret my parents wanted to tell me. And, sure enough, after we had venerated the Three Treasures, my father began to speak to me in whispers. "The Hawkens are *very* rich," he said.

"But we're rich, too, right?" I asked. "We make eight hundred dollars a month."

"The Hawkens make *thousands* of dollars a month," my dad told me.

"They make a thousand dollars a month?"

"No," said my father. "*Thousands* of dollars."

I simply had no conception of those kinds of numbers, and I was never convinced that they made more than a thousand. Since we got so much money by Green Gulch standards, it didn't occur to me that anybody could have much more than we did. I logically reasoned that if my family was given twice as much as everyone else, Baker Roshi and his family probably got about twice as much again, or $1,600 a month. (In reality, I think he got much more, but I didn't know that then.) A thousand dollars a month was about as much as I could imagine anyone other than Baker Roshi having, and I couldn't conceive of anyone getting more money than Baker Roshi.

Over the next days, weeks, months, and years the Hawkens lived with us, I was baffled by why they made so much money. It didn't make sense to me. Baker Roshi was the abbot. My father was the tanto. But the Hawkens weren't priests or even monks. They'd barely set foot on the path of enlightenment. So why did they make more money than my family?

Still, they lived in a trailer like everyone else, and they ate with us in the communal dining room. Mr. and Mrs. Hawken practiced Buddhism at the zendo. Occasionally they would tell us stories about other countries they had visited, but I didn't associate their travels with wealth or status. I assumed anyone could travel, and I found their stories entertaining, so I was willing to forgive them for making so much money.

Then, one day, I smelled sawdust just down the hill and walked over to investigate. I found the carpentry crew working on the foundation for an enormous building. As the building grew, I learned it was being built according to a Japanese carpentry technique that didn't require nails.

Soon it came out that the huge structure was going to be a house for the Hawken family. By American standards it was just a large house, but I would have had to leave Green Gulch and go to a prosperous suburban community to find one as big. If we could share the Bullpens with another family, the Hawkens could have shared this house with three.

Aidan bragged to me about how great their house was going to be. His mother, he confided, had told him it was going to have a secret passage but that we weren't supposed to mention that to his father because it was going to be a surprise.

Me on my bike, age nine. The Hawkens' house is being built in the background.

I assumed the house was a gift from the Board of Directors, just as our new car had been, and I wondered why they deserved it. It was one thing that the Hawkens had more money than my parents. They were from the Outside World, and I knew the rules were different there. However, I also knew the rules of Green Gulch. People got what they got according to merit. My father had been a Buddhist monk for almost fifteen years. He was a disciple of Shunryu Suzuki Roshi, who had been instrumental in bringing Zen to America.

The Hawkens may have been important in the Outside World, but at Green Gulch they were nothing more than laypeople and students who practiced under my father's administration. I didn't entirely like living with another family, even if they were in a separate wing. I'd been complaining that my room was too small. And now Aidan, his sister, and their parents were each going to get a room much larger than mine in a house they had all to themselves, even though my father, not theirs, was the tanto.

I learned later on that the Hawkens were paying for the house to be built out of their own pocket. But I still felt the whole project was inappropriate. Why was it so important to them to live better than the rest of us? They may have paid for the house, but the Zen Center owned the land. It wasn't until many years later that my father told me the Hawkens had been donating substantial sums of money to the Zen Center, and so, when they asked to pay for the house to be built, Baker Roshi had given them permission.

Fortunately for my pride, the house-building project was suddenly suspended. Something was up. I sensed more than understood a shift, or more accurately a vacuum of authority, at the Zen Center. The winds of power were changing. I began to hear stories. Then, in 1983, I learned that Baker Roshi had decided to walk from Green Gulch all the way to Tassajara, our retreat center far to the south of San Francisco. I'd driven there with my family, and I knew it was a colossal walk. More to the point, though, I realized that the community didn't want Baker Roshi around any longer, and that he didn't want to be around.

When he was confronted with his thefts and indiscretions, Baker Roshi denied everything. Finally the community condemned him, and he said he would walk to Tassajara to purify himself. However, my father has since told me that he was actually driven there by friends and had just made it appear that he'd walked. The outraged community finally asked him to leave, and he resigned in 1983 to avoid the humiliation of being kicked out.

Well after all this took place, I found out that my father had been one of the people responsible for uncovering all these improprieties. After Baker Roshi resigned, but before my family left Green Gulch, there was a debate in the community over who should succeed him as abbot. My father was one obvious candidate, but the tanto of the City Center, Reb Anderson, was also a likely choice. Although, as I've already discussed, my parents never really explained all their reasons for leaving Green Gulch, I think one deciding factor was that they'd become disillusioned by everything that had happened during those last few years.

My father was very upset by the scandal, and my mother felt betrayed and distressed. They didn't think the Hawkens should have been allowed to build their house, and, later on, my father came to realize that Baker Roshi hadn't given him the car and the raise in allowance because he thought my father had merited them. Rather, he'd been spreading the wealth as a way of rationalizing his own excesses. No doubt my father found that disillusioning as well. In any case, he decided to give up the opportunity to become the abbot and leave the Zen Center behind. Shortly after we left, Reb Anderson became the new abbot.

All this was disillusioning to me, too. I was only eight or nine at the time, so I didn't understand everything that was happening, but I was old enough to question why the Hawkens had been allowed to build their house on Green Gulch property. And my parents did tell me some of the things Baker Roshi had done (leaving out the sex scandal). I was shocked because he had been my ultimate Buddhist role model, and all of us kids had looked up to him.

In retrospect, knowing what I know now, I'm even more appalled. In my opinion, he did more than betray the trust of his female students. He desecrated our trust and betrayed our ideals by becoming the worst kind of materialist. Baker Roshi was a very charismatic leader, and many people had been seduced by his charm.

I still think the majority of people at Green Gulch legitimately believed in nonmaterialism, but seeing how quickly those ideals could become corrupted by hypocrisy was very upsetting to me. Ever since we left, I've carried with me many questions about materialism and nonmaterialism. Despite the hypocrisy at Green Gulch, I took with me a strong allegiance to the ideal of nonmaterialism, and, starting my new life in the American mainstream, I had to figure out how to live with that ideal in a materialistic world.

PERSONAL FINANCE AND COMMUNAL LIFE

Looking back on my naïveté with regard to the amount of money we received as a family at Green Gulch, and my inability to imagine anyone's earning more than a thousand dollars a month, I realize how poorly I was prepared by our communal lifestyle for making my way on the Outside. One important and practical skill I'd imagine most people in the Outside World have learned by the time they reach adulthood is how to manage personal finances. And, while I'm aware that, even in the Outside World, not everyone is a Wall Street wizard, it seems reasonable to assume that any kid who'd grown up hearing his parents discuss the rise and fall of the stock market, whose family owned or rented a home or were concerned with paying their monthly bills, would acquire some basic knowledge of day-to-day money management.

At Green Gulch, however, having a knowledge of personal finance was not considered important. At a practical level, because we were all provided with a roof over our heads, food, and a living allowance, no one had to worry about paying off a mortgage, coming up with rent money, or even earning a living. And, on an idealistic level, most members of the community looked upon any kind of interest in the stock market or financial investment as a form of materialism. They seemed to think that anyone who spent too much time thinking about money must not be spending enough time becoming enlightened.

So, I was raised to believe that understanding personal finance was not only unimportant but also materialistic. And, even after my family left Green Gulch, my parents didn't seem to think it was important to teach me very much about han-

dling money. Of course, they had to take care of their own finances. In fact, by 1988, just before I started my freshman
year in high school, they bought the house in Tam Valley
where they still live. But, despite their home-ownership, they
still maintained that, in the overall scheme of things, finance
was not very important and materialism was unenlightened.

Recently, however, I've come to realize that understanding
personal finance *is* important. For example, I'd like to buy a
house someday, and that will mean getting a bank loan and
paying off a mortgage. I've also learned the importance of in-
vesting for my future and thinking now about the security of
my later years. But I've had to learn practically everything I
know about personal finance on my own.

For me, the question of how to deal with money is part of
the conflict between materialism and nonmaterialism. If I get
too absorbed in money, the stock market, and accumulating
wealth, is it possible that I'll lose sight of the nonmaterial
things I consider more important? To me, life should be about
spiritual growth and caring for the welfare of others, but I realize that if I am to live in a world based on a free-market
economy, I'm also going to have to pay at least some attention
to securing my own position in that world. And so, the issue
for me remains how to stay true to my ideals without slighting
my attention to practical matters—and vice versa.

FINDING THE MIDDLE WAY

I can't go back to Green Gulch. It still exists as part of the San
Francisco Zen Center, and I've been back to visit several times

over the past few years, but, at the time of this writing, it's not really a commune anymore. It's still a monastery in the sense that it still has active monks, but I didn't get the sense, on my recent visits, that there were very many families living there. Nor did I get the impression that the monks were there to stay. I think most of them—and many are quite young—were there just to practice Buddhism for a few years before moving on to the next stage of their lives. The community I grew up in doesn't exist in the form it did then. I wouldn't be able to go back there to live an alternative way of life as my parents did, and, in that sense, I'm barred from that culture forever.

So I have to make my way in the Outside World. I now work as a computer programmer in Berkeley, California. I live in an apartment. I own a car. I have to deal in money and material goods. How do I remain a good Buddhist in that material world?

First of all, many Buddhist concepts are more about balance than they are about extremes. Materialism is just one extreme; starving is the other. It's clear to me that being a good Buddhist doesn't necessarily mean taking a vow of poverty. In the world where I now live, I have to pay the rent, pay the bills, and, arguably, own a car in order to survive. To do that, I need a job. And there are benefits to living the middle-class life. I wouldn't want to be struggling. My programming job pays reasonably well, and having a little extra money means that if my car breaks down, I can fix it; if I have a medical problem not entirely covered by my insurance, I can pay for it; and so on for all the necessities and niceties of daily life.

But that doesn't mean I've become materialistic or fallen victim to desire. It's really about survival. I think that in order to be a good Buddhist, I must keep sight of the things I believe are really important in life. I truly believe that material things cannot really make me happy. I may think they do when I buy them, but I believe that's just an illusion. The trick for me is to ask myself why I buy the things I do. I have to ask myself if what I'm buying is practical or whether I'm buying it just because I have the false sense that it will make me happy. If I buy a car, did I buy it for transportation or because it's safe and doesn't break down easily, or did I buy it so I could brag about it to my friends who don't have as nice a car as I do? (And what kind of friend would I be if I did that, anyway?) If I set a goal for myself to make $1,000,000 by the time I'm forty, how will I feel if I turn forty and haven't achieved that goal? And, if I did achieve it, how many friends, lovers, and life-enriching experiences would I have had to forgo in its pursuit?

I try not to look to material objects for happiness but to rely instead on things I find more enriching, but I don't always succeed. I'm by no means perfect. I may be on the path to enlightenment, but I'm not enlightened. There is one part of me that tries to be a good Buddhist and another part that isn't so good a Buddhist. Sometimes I fall into the materialist trap. It can be easy to do. Recently, I replaced my television with a new one, just because the new one was bigger. I see the same shows and I don't think having a bigger TV really does much to make me happier than when I had the smaller one, but it was easy to think it would at the time I bought it.

The real issue for me is how to judge, on a daily basis, whether buying something is materialistic or not. How do I distinguish between the things I need and the things to which

I'm too attached? Sometimes these determinations are easy. As should already be clear, anything I definitely need is not materialistic. I would also put practical things in the same category. Having a printer for my computer, for example, is, for me, very practical, even necessary.

But these determinations can be quite difficult. The best way to make them, I think, is to ask yourself how whatever it is you are intending to buy is going to fit into your life. If I think that simply having something is going to make me happy—as I did with the big TV—I judge that thing to be materialistic. If, however, there's some nonmaterial aspect of my life that will be enriched by my acquiring some material thing, if I can afford it, I'll usually buy it. For example, I wouldn't hesitate to buy a book about a subject that really interests me, because buying the book would help me to learn about that subject.

Of course, life for me is not always serious. I like to have fun and to be entertained as much as anyone else. But sometimes spending the afternoon talking with a friend can be worth much more than, say, watching a DVD alone on a new DVD player. When all else fails, I just try to keep track of the nonmaterial things that are really important to me, and when I do that, my decisions about buying material things naturally fall into place.

As far as personal finance goes, I think that spending too much time worrying about money and following my investments would be an unhealthy form of materialism. And I don't believe in risking my money on short-term investments because that would be a form of gambling. But, on the other hand, I don't think that taking an interest in one's own personal finance is *necessarily* materialistic. Making money is not my main goal in life, but I don't think there's anything wrong with keeping track of the money I do make. I don't think it's wrong to look forward to owning my own home, or, if I have children one day, to save money for their education. Those are both, to my mind, worthwhile goals that require prudent financial planning.

In the end, the way I've found the balance for myself is simply to do what I feel is important with my life. After that, my financial needs follow, and I try to manage my personal finances as best I can.

I think the most important thing right now is that I know what I believe in and I know how to live practically in the Outside World. I've seen the good and bad of both worlds and, because of that, I'm able to judge both sides and figure out how to take the best of both and live as a good, if not a perfect, Buddhist.

FIVE

PATIENCE VERSUS IMPATIENCE

I was on vacation with my family. I don't remember exactly
how old I was, but probably about seven or eight, because I
know we were still living at Green Gulch. My family didn't
have a lot of money, but my parents didn't believe in extravagant vacations anyway.

We were staying in a small town on the California coast.
One day my father and I decided to rent a tandem bicycle and
take a ride together. It was a beautiful day—the sky perfectly
clear, the sea air salty, and the sun warm on our backs.

It took more concentration to ride the tandem than we'd
thought. Since it was longer than a normal bicycle, it tipped
over more easily. It was even harder because there were two of
us, and one of us would sway one way while the other swayed
another until pretty soon the bicycle became unbalanced. It
took great coordination, too, because we both had to pedal at
the same speed. If one of us pedaled too fast, the bicycle went

too quickly, and if one of us pedaled too slowly, the other had to do too much work.

But I wasn't focused on riding the tandem, on how beautiful the day was, or on enjoying the time with my father. I wanted to talk about what we were going to do next. I listed all of the things I wanted to do on our vacation. I kept talking about everything except riding the tandem.

Finally, my father stopped me. "Ivan," he told me, "one of the things we believe in Buddhism is that you shouldn't think about the future all the time. The future hasn't happened yet, so we believe in thinking about the present, because it's what's happening right now. You're so busy talking about what you want to do next that you can't even enjoy taking this ride on this beautiful day. Why don't we try just to enjoy the ride?" I took my father's advice, and we had a wonderful time pedaling around the town.

PATIENCE AND THE SECOND NOBLE TRUTH

According to the Second Noble Truth, suffering is caused by desire. If you want something to happen faster than it's going to happen, that's impatience—and it's also desire. So, it logically follows that a Buddhist should learn to be patient. In fact, Zen meditation, which is the practice of sitting for a very long time with a straight back and not thinking about anything, could be described as an exercise in patience. Some Zen Buddhists, as I've said, practice meditation for a week or more at a time in what's known as a sesshin, pausing only to eat and sleep.

What my father told me about Buddhism during that vacation was true. The Buddha thought most people spent too much time thinking about the future and the past and not enough time just being in the present. If you think about it, being impatient means thinking too much about the future. The Buddha said that the past no longer exists and the future has not yet existed. In fact, our conceptions of the future are just what we *think* will happen. But we really don't know what will happen. The Buddha didn't say we should *never* think about the future, because, after all, we do sometimes have to make plans in order to live a practical life. But he did say that dwelling too much on what hadn't yet happened would be foolish, because if you hope something good will happen, it's possible that it won't happen, and if you're worried something bad will happen, it's possible that won't happen either.

Just a few months before this writing, I sat Zen meditation in the zendo of the Berkeley Zen Center. After sitting in the lotus position for half an hour, my feet had fallen asleep (which often happens when one sits in the lotus position for a long time), and it was hard for me to stand up. One of the priests who was responsible for monitoring Zen students and making sure they were meditating correctly came up to me and whispered that I should just be patient. "Just keep sitting," he said, "and the tingling will stop and then you can get up."

After a half hour of thinking nothing, part of me was glad it was over and wanted to get up immediately. I think that's human nature. Another part of me knew that being glad the meditation period was over was missing the point. Zen meditation is about letting go of our thoughts, feelings, and impatience, and just being. If I could just be for half an hour, I could just be for a few minutes more while I waited for my feet to wake up.

BEING PATIENT IN THE WORLD OUTSIDE

Green Gulch was always quiet and tranquil. The adults spent a good part of each day working on tasks that needed to be done around the monastery, but everybody took his or her time to do these tasks. No one was ever busy. People didn't procrastinate about getting their jobs done, but they never rushed, either.

So, my parents had always taught me to be patient. If I got impatient, they told me, "Things happen when they happen." They'd ask me why I wanted things to happen any sooner. They taught me not to rush and just to let things happen in their own time.

In the Outside World, it's just the opposite. The Outside World is always fast-paced, or at least it seems that way to me. People are worried about getting to work on time. They're worried about getting things done in time for their boss, or in time to make this sale or cut that deal. American culture abounds with phrases like "time is money" and "the early bird catches the worm."

In urban traffic jams, people honk their horns at one another because they're not getting where they want to go fast enough, or they're trying to find a shortcut that will get them to where they want to go sooner. Drivers cut me off on the road, try to go around me, tailgate me, all in the hope of getting past me.

And, who am I to say they're wrong? People *have* to get to work on time. If their boss sets a deadline, they have to make that deadline. If not getting a certain thing done by a certain time is bad for business, one has to get that thing done by that time. If one is late for something, whether it's a business appointment or a social engagement, there are generally bad consequences. So maybe in the Outside World, people have to rush. And, if people in the Outside World have to rush, doesn't that mean that I now have to rush too?

There have been times when being patient has not paid off for me. There have been times when I'm waiting for something and it doesn't happen immediately. Sometimes I'll be waiting for a table at a restaurant, and it will take a very long time for me to be seated. Is the waitperson not seating me because there are no tables or because he or she is taking advantage of my patience? Would I be seated faster if I kept asking when my table was going to be ready?

A few years ago, I placed a personals ad. A woman responded and we talked several times on the phone. She seemed like someone I'd want to meet, so I asked her if she'd like to have coffee with me sometime. We agreed to meet at a coffee shop we both knew and set a date and time.

I arrived on time. Fifteen minutes passed and she still hadn't shown up, but that didn't seem late to me. Maybe she was caught in traffic. Then, after half an hour, I started to worry that she wouldn't show up. I called her from a pay phone at the coffee shop and got her answering machine. I left a message telling her I was there, but I assumed that if she wasn't home, she was probably on her way. In the end, I spent an hour waiting at the coffee shop and then left.

That evening, I called and asked her what had happened. She told me she'd just forgotten, but she was so unapologetic I decided this woman wasn't worth being patient for.

In retrospect, I should have left after about twenty minutes. Well, I'm sure we've all done similarly stupid things in the course of our dating lives. I kept telling myself the woman would show up if I waited just a little longer. And I was also remembering what my parents had taught me about a good Buddhist's being patient. I now think that, on that particular occasion, I was *too* patient.

But it's not only when I'm waiting for people that I have to decide whether or not to be patient. What if something in my life isn't going my way fast enough? Should I work hard to make what I want happen or should I just be patient until it happens in its own good time?

Sometimes I'm waiting to hear news about something in my life. Will it be good news or bad news? If I see my doctor about some particular health problem and he runs tests, will it be good news or bad news? If I have some great opportunity in my life and I work hard to make the best of it, there's inevitably a period when I have to wait to see whether or not I'll get what I was hoping for. There have been times in my life's journey when I've decided to go down this path or that, and there's inevitably been someone or some organization acting as gatekeeper. It seems that there's always some period of time I have to wait to get what I want. Maybe there's a class I need to take, but none of the local schools are teaching it, at least at this time. When will the class be offered? Maybe I'm trying to find the right Buddhist congregation or the right Buddhist teacher, but those I find don't feel right to me. When will I find the right congregation or the right teacher?

If I follow my parents' teachings, I should logically wait indefinitely for people to return my calls, for medical tests to come back, for the right class to be offered at the right time, and so forth. American cultural mores, however, seem to dictate that I should get impatient after a while. Maybe at Green Gulch what my parents taught me about being patient worked better than it works in the Outside World. Maybe if nobody was rushing, but nobody was procrastinating either, I wouldn't have to worry about whether tasks got done in a timely manner, because I'd know that whatever the task, it would get done when it got done. Maybe at a place like Green Gulch, I could wait for someone to respond to me and know that I'd hear from him in time, because I'd be able to trust him to get the thing done in the time it took to do it. Maybe that trust would allow me to be patient. But maybe, without that trust, in the fast-paced Outside World, time *does* matter and I need to be a bit impatient in order to get things done before my life passes by.

Patience versus Impatience is a conflict because it seems to me that if I'm too patient, I might not be doing what I need to do in American culture. If I'm too impatient, however, that might mean I'm desiring too much. Does being impatient mean that I'm thinking about the future too much and not enough about the present?

FINDING THE MIDDLE WAY

Obviously, I can't wait forever for something I want or need. If I'm willing to wait indefinitely, I might be waiting a very long time. In American culture, being 100 percent patient simply isn't practical. But I don't think the Buddha really thought we should be 100 percent patient. It's true he thought we shouldn't spend too much time thinking about the future, but he didn't believe we shouldn't think about the future at all. If we think only about the present, we won't be able to live practically, and the whole point of the Middle Way is to find a means of living practically within the tenets of Buddhism.

There may be some ways being patient might serve me well in the context of American culture. Maybe if I'm waiting in a restaurant and I don't get seated right away, it's because the waitstaff needs some time to prepare my table. Maybe if somebody doesn't return my call as soon as I'd like, it's because he or she is really busy. Maybe if I rush my waitperson, he or she won't be able to do as good a job. Maybe if I nag somebody to return my phone call, it will put pressure on him to give me an answer before he's really prepared.

Maybe if I wait to meet the right teacher, the right woman, or the right group of people, I'll find a better match than I would if I settled for the first teacher, woman, or group I found. In those cases, being impatient would prevent me from thinking about what I'm doing in the present and force me to rush and maybe not get what I really wanted.

But, while it's true that one can make a Buddhist argument in favor of being patient, I think one can also make a Buddhist argument for being impatient under certain circumstances.

The Buddha said that everything in the universe is constantly changing, nothing lasts forever, and nothing is predictable except unpredictability. That's why he didn't think we should look to the future—because whatever we think will happen, and therefore base our plans on, may change.

But doesn't being too patient assume that the future is predictable? When I waited an hour for that young woman to show up for our coffee date, wasn't I being patient because I *assumed* she'd show up? If I've left a message on somebody's answering machine and I'm waiting indefinitely for him or her to return my call, doesn't that mean I think I can count on getting that return call?

Maybe what the Buddha really believed was that the answer doesn't lie in being either patient or impatient all the time. Maybe being too patient and too impatient both involve looking to the future too much. Since, as I've said, Buddhists don't always see the existence of opposites and contradictions in the same way Westerners do, this would be a perfectly logical Buddhist conclusion.

In fact, it may be that sometimes when I'm patient about one thing, I'm ironically being impatient about another. Maybe when I waited so long to meet the woman at the coffee shop, it was because I was impatient about meeting women. Clearly, she wasn't the right woman for me, so maybe if I had been more patient about meeting the right woman, I would have had an easier time leaving the coffee shop.

And maybe never looking to the future is just as big a problem as always looking to the future. While it's true that if one looks to the future one may forget to enjoy the ride, if one never looked to the future, one would never make plans or see what might be coming up ahead. And, for that reason, I don't think that looking to the future from time to time is at all un-Buddhist. I think that when the Buddha said we shouldn't spend all our time looking to the future, he also meant we shouldn't spend all our time just thinking about the present.

How, then, do I know when to be patient and when to be impatient? Maybe it's just like riding the tandem bicycle with my father. It's important to enjoy the ride, but it's also important to look far enough down the road to prevent yourself from crashing. So, if I think I'm going to be nagging the waitstaff too much to seat me immediately in a restaurant, maybe I should be more patient. That would be enjoying the ride. But, if I look ahead and see that my needs might not be met if I don't follow up on a telephone call, maybe it's time to be a little more impatient.

I think that if I really want something in my life to happen and it's not happening as fast as I'd like, I should be patient long enough to see if things are going my way. But, if I wait a long time and things aren't going my way, I also think it's okay to be impatient enough to take the initiative to make things happen.

Patience and impatience are encapsulated in Buddhism by the acts of meditating and ceasing to meditate. Zen meditation is the ultimate act of patience, because it is the practice of simply being in the present. Ceasing meditation and getting on with your life is impatience in the sense that it turns once again to the future. Sometimes, I don't always know whether I should be patient or impatient, but when I meditate, I clear my mind of all thoughts and emotions. When I finish meditating I'm usually calm. So, there's always one simple test I know will help me to decide whether to be patient or impatient. I can meditate, and if I'm still impatient when I stop, I think it's *good* for me to be impatient, but if I'm patient, I think I should continue to be patient.

While I realize that not everyone will find their answer to this problem in meditation, I do think that—like most things in life—finding the Middle Way with relation to patience and impatience requires considering the particular circumstances and deciding which path will best serve one's interests without violating one's principles in any given instance.

SIX

CHILD CARE VERSUS CHILD FREEDOM

Although my father was not generally directly involved in our child-care arrangements, I remember one Sunday when he came to the child-care center to give us a lesson in Buddhist practices.

At the time, child care was held in one room of a small building that sat at the top of a cliff to one side of the gulch. In the middle of the room was a wrestling mat on which we kids liked to do somersaults and cartwheels, and for that reason, we called the child-care room the Tumbling Room.

My father asked us to sit quietly in a circle on the mat. Then he told us to count our breaths from one to ten. When we got to ten, he said, we should start over at one. He explained that this was Zen meditation and what people did in the zendo.

We sat quietly for a few minutes and breathed. Then, one of the older boys started joking that he could see all these

My father and I in our front yard.

Buddhas floating in the clouds. Soon, more of the kids started laughing and joking around. Even I laughed, just to prove I was cool.

Until that day, with the exception of the stories that were read to us on Buddha's Birthday, we'd never had a formal lesson in Buddhist practice. Perhaps we should have been told about the lesson in advance; perhaps it should have been held in a more formal setting; or perhaps it was simply too little too late. My father had hoped to start a kind of Sunday school and teach us something about Buddhism each week. But, whatever was the reason for our inability to take him seriously, he quickly became frustrated, and that was the first and last formal, Sunday school–style lesson in Buddhism we ever had.

• • •

The Green Gulch community taught me a lot of wonderful values, and I'm proud of growing up there. But, as I hope I've been making clear all along, not everything at Green Gulch was good. One thing that was seldom good was the way the adults took care of the children. The adults made great role models for us because they were devout Buddhists. But, in my opinion, they didn't take proper care of their greatest treasure—the next generation of Buddhists.

At any given time during my years there, at least a dozen children lived at Green Gulch, and there were many more whose parents practiced their Buddhism at Green Gulch but didn't actually live on campus. The problem was that our child-care system really wasn't very good. The people in charge weren't professionals, and we children weren't always supervised. But what we particularly lacked was any kind of formal Buddhist education.

There's an old Zen joke that goes: How many Zen Buddhists does it take to change a light bulb? The answer is: Two. One to do it and one to not do it.

One principle of Zen is that every statement or concept contains its opposite. Mathematicians hold a similar concept in set theory. They call it "the empty set." Any set, no matter how many subsets it may have, also has as a subset the empty set, or a subset that is nothing at all. From a Zen perspective, then, non–child care, which I'm calling child freedom, is part of the subject of child care. By child care, I don't mean only organized day care but rather all the ways adults take care of children, including parental involvement and the relationship of all the adults in the community with the children of that community. By child freedom I mean not only our freedom to roam the eighty acres of Green Gulch, but also the lack of adult supervision, even a certain carelessness (or lack of caring) in the way we children were treated by many of the adults there.

Our child-care system was supposed to be run like professional child-care programs and provide a safe place where parents could drop off their children and know they would be taken care of. Unlike professional child-care programs, however, the one at Green Gulch was run by volunteers, and we children often had to be there for more than just a few hours. The ideal, at least from our parents' perspective, was that we would be in child care whenever we were not in school and they were in the zendo. Child care was supposed to be daily during the summer and also in the afternoons and on weekends when school was in session. But, as I've said, our child-care program did not always live up to that ideal.

From the time the first children were born or arrived at Green Gulch, people in the community argued about what to do with us. Unfortunately, many Buddhist students (both monks and laypeople) perceived us as nothing more than a noisy and undisciplined distraction from their studies and practice.

I've sometimes tried to imagine what it must have been like for a monk taking a meditative dinner in the dining room with us kids forever running underneath the tables, playing on the chairs, and dashing from one end of the room to the other. Or, the monk might be meditating in the zendo, trying to count his breaths while, just outside, some child would be about to tag another, the second would squeal in mock fear, and the sound would interrupt the monk in mid-breath and tear his mind back to conscious thought.

We children were always running when we should have walked, or rushing from room to room rather than staying in one place. We'd dash through the gaitan in our muddy shoes when we should have walked across the floor in bare feet. In short, we were constantly disrespecting the sanctity of the monastery and breaking the rules.

A monk might try to ignore us, he might try to vote down any suggestion that would put the kids' interests first, or he might vote for a mediocre child-care program just to keep us from interrupting his Buddhist meditation and practice. However, a monk could also have an entirely different reaction. Meditation, after all, is supposed to help a person become more accepting of the things that come into his world—such as children making noise. So, one might say that a monk, in particular, ought to be understanding of childlike behavior and accept it as normal and natural—especially the monks at Green Gulch, who were, after all, converts who'd grown up on the "Outside" and had, presumably, run around and made noise as children themselves.

Personally, I believe that nothing can interrupt a truly clear mind. Now, when I hear children yelling outside while I'm meditating, I always smile. If I can learn to meditate though loud noises, I think my meditation can really become pure.

WHERE CHILD CARE FAILED

Most of the parents at Green Gulch no doubt wanted a good child-care program. But most of the students, who didn't have children, threw their weight against child care in one way or another. Some of them wanted as little child care as possible, perhaps because they hoped to conserve community resources for other purposes. Others simply wanted to establish rules that would keep the children out of sight, hearing, and mind.

What emerged from this debate was that the community established an on-campus child-care program of sorts. Unfortunately, however, it never really worked as well as had been intended.

When I first arrived at Green Gulch, child care wasn't held in the Tumbling Room. It was in an old corral just down the hill from the Bullpens and uphill from the residential parking lot, which held several wooden climbing structures and a tepee. Every day we started by gathering in the teepee with the person in charge to sing songs and participate in other group activities. In many ways, the teepee was the focal point of the child-care area, and we called the corral the Teepee Yard.

The person in charge of child care changed often during my early childhood, and I later learned it was a job taken up on a volunteer basis. Taking charge of child care was no more popular than kitchen duty, and I never had the sense that there were any qualifications for it, either. Perhaps people simply stopped doing child care whenever they got tired of it and a new person would have to volunteer.

There were always parts of the day or days in the week—

even when we weren't in school—that we didn't have child care at all. At those times we simply got together and wandered all over Green Gulch doing whatever we chose. Sometimes we were in sight of one or more adults and sometimes we weren't. There were times when we fought and there was no authority figure around to help us settle the dispute.

We did, however, have a long list of rules, including "no screaming in the Central Area" (the grassy lawn at the center of Green Gulch) and "no running on the Upper Deck," which were intended to protect the tranquillity of Buddhist practice. Unfortunately, they also prevented us from acting like normal kids. We weren't allowed to make noise, and we were discouraged—not always successfully—from playing in centers like the dining room, near the zendo, or on the central lawn.

Our response to these restrictions was not to play in the areas where adults congregated. Instead, we went behind this building or between those. We often took off into the hills or into creek gullies. There was a little trail that went from the dining room area, under a row of plum trees, around the mail room, and out to the central lawn. If we were scolded for running around in front of the dining room, we could escape to the lawn area. If we were told, "No screaming in the Central Area," we could slip away to the Wheelwright Center.

Often, we'd be shooed out of each place by a different group. One group might be attending a lecture in the Wheelwright Center while another was having tea on the lawn. We'd then disappear from the adults altogether, perhaps sliding down the golden grass that grew above the fields on cardboard sheets we'd stolen from the recycling bins behind the kitchen.

● ● ●

The community did set aside one room, known as the Family Room, especially for the children. It was furnished with couches, giant stuffed animals, beanbags, toys, and a loft. It also had a sink and a counter where bread, jam, peanut butter, crackers, and fruit were always laid out. It was there that we went to play after dinner, out of the way of the dutiful monks and students who wanted to enjoy their meal in peace.

The Family Room is the only place I can remember, apart from the Teepee Yard or the Tumbling Room, that was specifically for children, and it was the only communal area where an entire family could spend time together, alone or with other families.

Despite this fact, however, families almost never used it. I remember going to friends' houses and doing things with my family at home, but I don't remember an entire family ever spending time together in the Family Room *as* a family. In fact, I rarely saw parents in the Family Room at all. The adults usually stayed in the dining room to socialize after meals, or they spent that time practicing Buddhism—meditating, chanting, or studying.

I particularly recall one occasion when I was playing with a group of children in the Family Room after dinner. All the adults were either still in the dining room or in the kitchen washing up. A girl named Robin was playing with a large red plastic ball that was covered with various holes and had a giant needle attached to it with a plastic cord. The needle could be woven through the holes in various ways. Robin, however, soon became bored weaving. Suddenly, she was swinging the ball around her head. The cord was so long that the ball's orbit filled the entire room.

The rest of us took cover behind the couches and chairs or crouched in the corners as Robin terrorized us with her flailing. It made me angry. It wasn't fair that she could fill up the whole space with her play. Worst of all, she was endangering the rest of us. We all yelled at her to stop, but she wouldn't.

I knew that if any of us came inside the radius of that ball, we'd get hurt, but I also wanted to stop her. I waited until the ball had just passed me. Then I jumped over the couch and ran at Robin. That's when the ball pegged me in the eye. I began to cry, and, at that point, some adults who'd been nearby must have heard me because they came to see what was happening. But the problem was that they hadn't been there to begin with. No one was supervising our play. If they had, the whole incident would never have occurred in the first place. Instead, the burden of resolving the conflict had rested with us children.

WHEN CHILD CARE DIDN'T FAIL

In every yin there's a dot of yang. If Green Gulch parents didn't generally spend much time with their children outside the home, there were times when they played a positive role in the community.

I remember, for example, that my mother, for whatever reason, was uncharacteristically unavailable to take me to the first day of nursery school. Instead, the father of another Green Gulch child, named Anna (the girl who had painted her lunch box), took us both. Anna's father was going to read her a story before he left for the day, and he must have noticed that I appeared a bit nervous, because he asked if I'd like to hear it, too. When I said I would, he took us both into a small room with a little playhouse in it and a shelf full of children's books. Anna and I picked the book we wanted, and he sat down on the carpet with us to read. Although I would have much preferred my mother to be there, it was comforting to have a familiar Green Gulch parent taking care of me on my first day in a strange new environment.

Most of the parents at Green Gulch were, in fact, very caring, and I certainly never felt neglected by my own parents. When school was in session, my mother gave up the early morning meditation session to stay home and see me off. And she was almost always at home when I returned. My father also spent time with me whenever he was able to get away from his duties as tanto.

Together, they guided me in life and taught me basic Buddhist values. I've already mentioned the time my mother taught me a lesson in the deceptive lure of popular culture when she bought me the Luke Skywalker action figure. But there were other, similar occasions, and I remember a particular incident that occurred when I was perhaps five. My parents had let me have some cookies, and I kept begging them for more even though my mother insisted I'd had enough. When I whined that I wanted more anyway, my father told me sternly that I couldn't always have what I wanted in life. He said that if I always wanted another cookie, I'd never be happy with the cookies I'd already eaten, but if I learned to be content with the cookies I received, I'd be able to take pleasure in them. He explained that the same was true for a lot of things in life. If I always wanted more, he told me, I'd never be satisfied, but if I learned to be content with the good things life brought me, I'd be allowing those things to make me happy. I see now that he was, in effect, explaining the Second Noble Truth in terms a five-year-old could understand.

There were also times when my mother became the caregiver for all the children in the community. Twice a year, Green Gulch held a weeklong meditation retreat or sesshin, as it's called in Japanese. It wasn't a retreat in the sense that anyone went away, but when the monks and laypeople "sat sesshin," they retreated from the practical areas of the monastery and spent most of each day meditating in the zendo. They would wake up early in the morning, go to the zendo, meditate, have breakfast, meditate some more, eat lunch in silence, meditate all afternoon, have a quiet dinner, meditate in the evening hours, then go to bed.

It was difficult for parents to sit sesshin and still spend time with their children. It was also hard to find people to volunteer for child care during sesshin. As a solution, my mother organized camping trips for the children during this time. With the help of two or three other volunteers, she took us up into the mountains where we slept in tents, had cookouts, and went hiking. We got to have things we were rarely allowed, such as little boxes of junk cereal for breakfast. In the evenings, we roasted s'mores around the campfire. We had a wonderful time, but I have to say that these kinds of special events were the exception rather than the rule.

The year I turned nine, my mother said she wanted to sit the winter sesshin with the rest of the community. She told me I

First kids' camping trip at Green Gulch. Left to right: my mother, me, and Hillary, a teenage Green Gulch girl.

was a big boy and could take care of myself. All that week, she snuck out of the zendo to wake me up and get me off to school. She was often meditating when I came home, but she did take the time to have a quick dinner with me at the Bullpens. (My father couldn't even take the time for dinner because his position meant that the community looked to him for leadership during the sesshin.)

At the end of that week, I hiked down the long dirt drive-way from where the school bus dropped me off at the side of Highway 1. I followed it past the guest parking lot through the eucalyptus trees, past the Wheelwright Center, and up an in-cline to the residential parking lot. From there, I ascended the hill via a flight of wooden stairs, crossed the splintery planks of the little bridge that spanned the creek, and made my way along the path to the Bullpens. I knew my mother wouldn't be home until that evening. It had been a hard week, and I was glad it was over. I mounted the porch on our side of the house, set my backpack on the worn, green couch, and went to my room.

There was my small loft and the little particleboard cubbies where I kept my toys. The room was so crowded that at first I didn't notice the large box on the floor in front of my loft.

"Did you see your present?" my mother's voice asked from behind me.

I turned around, and there she was, in jeans and a black turtleneck. She was still wearing her rakusu, the rectangular piece of cloth, about a foot square, that laypeople wore around their neck as a symbolic representation of the Buddha's robe.

"Mom," I exclaimed in surprise.

She gave me a hug. Then I turned back into my room and

grabbed the box, which contained race cars and track parts I could assemble. Since I normally received presents only on Christmas and my birthday, I was very excited.

I wasn't used to being without my mother. The race car set didn't replace her, but when she gave it to me, I knew she understood how difficult the separation had been for me, and that it had been hard for her, too. The gift wasn't a bribe. If she'd given it to me at the beginning of the week, it would have meant that she felt she needed to placate me for her absence. If she'd told me beforehand that I was going to get it, provided I was good, it would have implied that she was paying me off. Instead, it was a reward. I'd allowed her to do something for herself without asking anything in return and without complaining. The gift showed me that this had meant a lot to her.

As I've said, the people in charge of child care were always volunteers, and the job changed hands with some frequency. As you would expect, some of these people were better with children than others. One of my fondest memories is of a man named Tom, a man with a sincere and compassionate heart and the integrity to try to do what he thought was best for us kids.

He introduced us to the concepts of warm fuzzies, cold pricklies, and plastic fuzzies. Warm fuzzies are things one person does to another that feel good. Cold pricklies are things one person does that make someone else feel bad. Plastic fuzzies are things one person does that might at first feel good to the other person but that are, in fact, intended to hurt in a roundabout way.

These metaphors for human interactions might sound corny to adults, but we were children and we were hearing about them for the first time. If you imagine that throughout most of your childhood your social interactions with the other children in your community had been difficult and strained, you'll have some idea of how thoughtful Tom's concepts really were.

Each day, one kid became the warm fuzzy king or queen, and everyone else practiced giving that person warm fuzzies. We'd pile up pillows to make a throne for the designated child. Then, once he or she was comfortably seated, we'd each think of a warm fuzzy to give that person. At first we thought of physical things, such as a massage, but we soon learned that we could also give warm fuzzies in other forms, such as compliments.

Buddhism teaches compassion for all living beings, and I think Tom's metaphors really helped our social development. Learning to perform these simple acts of kindness eased us out of our deeply entrenched bickering and fighting and slowly but surely taught us how to be nicer to one another.

RELIGIOUS EDUCATION: A MODEST PROPOSAL

I think American Buddhists can learn a lot from the child-rearing mistakes that were made at Green Gulch. Other religions offer some good models that I think Buddhists can look to for structuring the rearing of Buddhist children. Although I don't have much firsthand experience with Sunday school in a church setting, it appears to me to be a good model for receiving formal religious education. Maybe Buddhist children could be taught Buddhist stories—like the story of the life of the Buddha that we were taught on Buddha's Birthday—at an early age and be taught the basics of Buddhist philosophy (which is a bit complicated for very young children) at an older age. I'm sure that if American Buddhists put their heads together they could come up with a "Sunday school" curriculum that would work for Buddhist children.

Another model would be the way Jewish children are taught about their religion. When I was a child, both during my Green Gulch years and after, I was a good friend of several Jewish children who were not affiliated with our community, and I noticed that much of their religious upbringing occurred in the home. Perhaps another way for Buddhist children to learn about their religion is in the home. While we were at Green Gulch, I know there were situations my parents used as opportunities for teaching me lessons in Buddhism on a practical level, but that was when we were living in a self-contained Buddhist community. Since these kinds of communities no longer exist in the same way, it seems to me even more important now for parents to teach Buddhist tenets at home.

During middle school, I attended the bar and bat mitzvahs of several of my friends. These services mark the passage of boys and girls to man- or womanhood. The child is required to lead a portion of the service and to read a lengthy passage from the Old Testament in Hebrew. Typically, children prepare at least a year for this day, and the preparation ensures that they acquire a fundamental knowledge of their religion. I think it would be wonderful if we American Buddhists could establish a similar rite of passage that would require a certain amount of formal religious training.

I understand that changes have already occurred at the San Francisco Zen Center, and that Buddhist child-rearing practices have improved significantly since I was a child at Green Gulch. So, perhaps some of my ideas are already being implemented. I hope that's true, and I hope that we Buddhists never give up on our Buddhist children.

FINDING THE MIDDLE WAY

For the most part, I believe, we needed more child care and less child freedom at Green Gulch. In a way, we lacked the most positive form of freedom: the freedom to play and be children in the areas, both domestic and religious, that were most important to the monastery. Disturbing as it may have been to the monks for us to play near the zendo, we *needed* to be near the zendo, and we should have been allowed to go into it. The zendo was the center of our religion, and yet we were constantly being chased away from it.

In writing this book, I have almost never doubted my credentials. I grew up in an American Zen Buddhist monastery. I was raised Buddhist and I learned a great deal about Buddhism through observing, asking questions, and simply living every day around adults who practiced it. Looking back at my childhood, however, I realize that very little of my Buddhist upbringing involved formal education. I wish I'd learned about Buddhism more formally. It would have been great to have been told Buddhist stories when I was little (other than

My father and I in a wooden hot tub located in the Bullpens.

on Buddha's Birthday) and to be able to discuss ethical and philosophical issues as I grew older. But, unfortunately, except for our one day a week of "Sunday school," there was almost no time when an adult other than my parents actually sat me or the other kids down to teach us what our religion was all about.

I recently met a Japanese Zen monk who was raised in a Zen Buddhist monastery in Japan. When I told him I'd grown up at Green Gulch but wasn't formally taught very much about Buddhism, he said, "You know more than you think." And I believe that's true. I learned a lot about Zen Buddhism even without being formally taught.

In part, I learned by observing. I was immersed from birth in the sights and sounds of the Buddhist monastery, first at the San Francisco Zen Center and then at Green Gulch. I observed the monks and laypeople as they were meditating and learned that sitting quietly was an activity the community valued. I heard their chants so many times that I practically memorized them—although I didn't always know what they meant.

I also asked a lot of questions. I remember, for example, asking my father about words from the Heart Sutra that the adults chanted daily. The chant goes like this:

No eyes.
No ears.
No nose.
No tongue.
No body.
No mind.
No color.
No sound.
No smell.
No taste.
No touch.

I asked him if the chant was about a ghost, because a ghost was the only thing I could think of that didn't have eyes, ears, body, mind, color, and so on. My father laughed and said, "Something like that." But he later explained that the passage strips away each of the chanter's sensory organs, and then the senses, one by one. Its purpose is the same as that of Zen meditation, to empty the mind.

I suppose it would have been possible for me not to have asked questions and simply to have observed the formalities without learning what they meant. But I can't really imagine myself, or any other child in the community, spending so much time among these rituals, teachings, and customs without at least some of them taking hold.

In spite of learning without being taught, however, I'm still resentful of the lack of effort devoted to child rearing at Green Gulch. As the years pass, it's become clear that Buddhism in America is neither a fad nor a form of rebellion. It's not something people practice just to spite their Christian or Jewish parents. Rather, it's a religion in its own right.

People join cults or become fans of bands like the Grateful Dead to escape or rebel against traditional society, but religion is a tradition in itself. And traditions thrive by being passed on from one generation to the next. The Green Gulch attitude toward child care, however, seemed antithetical to that goal. By shooing us away from central areas, the adults communicated to us that we weren't invited to be part of mainstream life. And the fact that child care went only halfway told us we were only halfway important, or that we were important only half the time.

Although all of our parents may have been involved in the nurturing of their own children, the majority of people in the community were not involved or invested in the work of nurturing the next generation of American Buddhists. I don't know why the adults at Green Gulch weren't more serious about involving the next generation. I wish they had been. In certain ways, their semi-sincerity about us implied a semi-sincerity about Buddhism as well.

It seems to me now that they were all so excited about celebrating their own freedom of religion that they were unable to see beyond their personal choices to the new tradition they had founded. But if Buddhism is to continue as an American religion, I believe we Buddhists need to find ways to care for our children and pass on our beliefs so that the tradition will be carried forward to successive generations.

SEVEN

NONVIOLENCE VERSUS VIOLENCE

I remember my first dinner at Green Gulch very clearly. I'd finished the salad on my plate. My mother sat across the red-and-white–checked tablecloth from me amidst a sea of tables, chairs, and strangers. At three-and-a-half years old, I was scared, but I was also excited to be embarking on this new adventure and ready for the challenge.

I got up from the table before my mother could stop me, and, dodging around a maze of table legs, exploded out of the dining room and into a small side room that would later become the Family Room. Two boys were already there, both of them bigger than I was.

"Hi," I greeted them. "I'm Ivan."

"I'm Micah," said the bigger one.

"I'm Sean," said the other.

Then, as soon as they'd closed their mouths and drawn a new breath, both boys attacked me, hitting me like an avalanche so that I was knocked to the floor. They continued to pummel me until a grown-up came into the room and yelled at them to stop.

At Green Gulch, people took the Buddhist belief in compassion for all living things to mean that we should be pacifists, and we kids were taught that war, violence, anger, and aggression (not only physical, but also verbal and emotional aggression) were wrong. The adults didn't think violence was ever a solution, no matter what the problem. Rather, they believed that all conflicts could be resolved through communication so long as one tried to treat oneself and others equally and fairly. In fact, they were such extreme pacifists that one could describe their beliefs as almost Gandhi-esque.

So why, in a place that was supposed to foster pacifism, did Micah and Sean meet me with such unprovoked aggression? Maybe they were simply bullies who liked to pick on younger kids, but I think the answer is more complicated than that. I believe the Green Gulch culture bred a fear of outsiders into us children. I don't think our parents or the other adults meant to teach us to be frightened or intolerant of others, but for us kids, Green Gulch was in many ways almost tribal in its insularity. Throughout my childhood there, we often had a sense that the Outside World was an unenlightened place, and we saw it as bad and dangerous. Therefore, it seems to me that when I arrived that evening, these two four-year-olds may have identified me as an outsider and been afraid of me. Perhaps it was their fear that caused their aggressive behavior.

• • •

As the result of my upbringing, the question of how we American Buddhists should handle the issue of violence and nonviolence, and how we can impart our beliefs to the next generation, is one of profound importance. It's one thing, I've learned, to preach nonviolence and quite another to deal with aggression on a day-to-day basis.

First of all, I want to make it clear that I'm not just talking about physical violence. To me the word violence encompasses conflict in all its forms, from a simple argument or disagreement to a physical fight to out-and-out war. By violence, I mean any action one person takes that is intended to be cruel or to hurt another. On a personal level, such an action could range from raising one's voice in an argument to yelling or swearing to punching or kicking, or even an armed attack. I don't think anyone would argue with the fact that, if someone hits you and you hit back, that's a violent response. But I also believe that if someone raises his voice to you, and you raise yours in response, that, too, is a violent response.

All my life, I've thought about what kinds of reactions would be appropriate to what I'm calling violent actions. When someone does something that makes me angry, how should I react? When I feel intimidated, how should I respond? Should I react violently, should I "take it lying down," or is there some third alternative? The ideals of nonviolence and pacifism may sound simple in principle, but their practical applications can be difficult.

At Green Gulch, I was surrounded by nonviolent ideals. People were always talking about antiwar demonstrations; how they'd avoided the draft in the Vietnam War era; their fears that, if there were another war, the draft might be reinstated; and the dangers of nuclear warfare.

I remember one night in the dining room when I was about six and some other kids told me about the draft. They'd probably overheard the adults discussing the issue. In any case, they told me that the next time there was a war, we'd all be drafted. I recall walking along the path behind the laundry room the next day thinking about military service and being really scared. When I shared my fears with my parents, they assured me that, even if there were a draft, I wouldn't have to worry about it until I was eighteen. But that didn't really stop me from worrying. Childhood fears are not always rational, kids don't have a very good sense of time, and I knew that I'd be eighteen one day.

On another occasion—I must have been eight or nine at the time—I heard the adults talking about a nuclear arms protest in which they were going to march, and I told my parents I wanted to go along.

We gathered with many other protesters in a park in San Francisco. People held up signs and we started marching into the street. As we moved along, others joined us until our lines stretched from one side of the street to the other. While we walked, we chanted, "One, two, three, four, we don't want a nuclear war. Five, six, seven, eight, we don't want to radiate." Eventually we came to a large square in front of a city building where someone spoke to us about the dangers of nuclear war. At the end of the day, my feet were as sore as they'd ever been, but I felt good about having protested something to which I was so strongly opposed. I was inspired by the conviction that all war is wrong, and I be-

Green Gulch adults and kids gathered together on Easter.

lieved that violence was always bad and to be avoided whenever possible.

That was the Green Gulch ideal, but in my daily interactions with my peers, that ideal, more often than not, fell by the wayside. Like any other kids, we played cowboys, cops, and soldiers. And no matter how many times the adults told us guns and violence were bad, we continued to "shoot" one another.

One day, I remember, I was with Sean, Micah, and a couple of other boys in the carpentry shed making wooden swords. As we nailed the small wooden hand guards to the wooden blades, Sean told us about karate, explaining the differences among white belts, brown belts, and black belts. After that, we

131

all started begging our parents to let us take karate lessons.

After much debate about the ethics of Zen Buddhist kids taking martial arts classes, the adults finally agreed that it would be acceptable for us to study aikido because it teaches only defense techniques that use the attacker's energy against him and doesn't include any attack forms. Sean and Micah signed up immediately. Then several other Green Gulch kids joined the same class, and shortly after, I joined, too.

In retrospect, I think the aikido class was a good experience. Not only did it bring us together, it also taught us that we could defend ourselves without hurting another person, and it helped us to learn that we could stand up for ourselves without being mean to one another. What it didn't do, however, was teach us to be more accepting of outsiders, and that's where our tendency to respond with aggression and anger remained the most evident.

One evening, I was sitting with the other kids in the dining room. I was six at the time, Sean and Micah were seven, and the oldest boy, Dion, was seven and a half. The woman who was then in charge of child care came over to our table with two young boys, five and eight. The older one stood proudly next to her with a puffed-out chest and a face that beamed exuberance, while the younger boy hid shyly behind her.

"Everybody," she said, "I want you to meet Julian and his little brother, Sam. They've just moved to Green Gulch and I'd like you to welcome them."

Suddenly, Dion started laughing out loud at Julian. Then Sean and Micah laughed, and Robin and I joined in. I didn't know why we were laughing at the new kids; in fact, I felt bad for Julian and Sam, but I wanted to be accepted by my peers and thought of as one of the tribe. In fact, I was doing to the new kids exactly what Sean and Micah had done to me on my first day at Green Gulch, except that I wasn't actually beating them up.

After dinner, my mother scolded me for my behavior.

"Julian and Sam are new here," she said, "and they were probably a little frightened to come. I think it would be nice if you invited them over to our house tonight."

"Do I have to?" I whined. I didn't want the other kids to reject me just because I was friends with the new kids, which they surely would have considered a betrayal of loyalties.

"I'd like you to," my mother insisted. "You never know, you guys might have a lot in common."

So, Julian and Sam came over to the Bullpens. As we leaned against the fence surrounding our yard, I told Julian how much I liked dinosaurs. As it turned out, Julian was also interested in dinosaurs, and he knew more about them than I did. He also liked tigers. He knew every variety of tiger on earth, from the small Bengal to the gigantic white Siberian. I was impressed.

Julian was a nice kid and, being two years older than I was, he knew a lot of things I didn't. Until then, I'd always thought of older kids as being standoffish. They never wanted to include me, and as one of the youngest, I was always among the first to be rejected. Julian, however, seemed to accept me and take me under his wing. We soon became close friends.

At first, things were fine. I played with Julian and Sam and continued to get along with Sean, Micah, and the others. After a while, however, Julian started talking about "war." He said we (he, Sam, and I) were a gang, and Dion and the other kids were another gang. The three of us built a wooden fort behind his family's trailer and started stockpiling weapons. We raided the carpentry shed for the longest boards we could find and made them into rubber-band guns with nails at one end to hold the rubber bands and safety pins at the other to let them fly. We made wooden swords and dirt clods. Soon we had a stack of rubber-band guns, a rack of swords, and a pile of dirt clods concealed in our "secret base."

Eventually we were joined by a fourth kid named Timmy, who was also young and had had problems being accepted by the older kids. Julian told us that someday soon we were going to have a war with the rival gang. He said they had their own secret base and their own cache of weapons. He said he was going to talk to Dion and the two of them would decide the time and place, probably somewhere the adults wouldn't see us. He made us all drill and prepare for that never-specified date.

The idea scared me. Not only was I afraid of getting hurt; I also truly believed that war was bad. So, one night I told my parents what Julian had planned. My father promised he'd talk to Julian for me, and, the next day, while the four of us sat rolling dirt clods in a mud puddle halfway between the Bullpens and Julian's trailer, my dad walked past us on the path and asked casually, "You're not going to hurt anybody with those, are you?"

"Oh, no," Julian assured him with a phony smile. "We're just playing with dirt. We just like to roll dirt in the mud."

"Okay, then," my father said, not really believing him. "As long as you don't hurt anybody, that's okay."

All that summer, the tension mounted. We kept on stock-piling weapons, and Julian kept hinting of the war that was to come. When we saw Dion's gang we exchanged dirty looks. At child care and dinner there was a good deal of posturing. Any inroads I'd made into being accepted by Dion's group were now totally gone.

Then one day when Timmy and I arrived for a meeting with Julian and Sam, we discovered that the fort behind their trailer had been completely destroyed. The clubhouse was knocked over, our wooden swords were broken, and the remains of dirt clods were scattered all over the place. Dion and his friends had somehow found out where our fort was and made a raid on it.

The feud never got more violent than that. Perhaps some of Julian's talk had been bluster, a fantasy he'd concocted to impress us. It's possible the war was never supposed to happen. And, even if it had, I don't think any of us was really planning to hurt the members of the rival gang. We'd probably just have shot rubber bands at one another, thrown a few dirt clods, and maybe banged our wooden swords together. But, for whatever reason, the war never came.

Although some people might be surprised that this kind of brinkmanship took place at a pacifist Zen monastery, I think it was no more than normal behavior for kids—particularly boys—in any environment. And, however much our parents told us guns, violence, and war were bad, they didn't supervise us closely enough to help us solve our conflicts in any other way.

When it comes to the issue of violence and nonviolence, the fundamental dilemma derives from the simple fact that conflict exists. The Green Gulch culture may have embraced nonviolence, but it also created strained social dynamics. As a result, it begged the question: How should we deal with conflict when it occurs? We may not live with conflict every moment of our lives, but in all our lives there are, have been, and always will be moments when conflict arises and strains in relationships develop. And when that happens, children in particular are likely to turn to violent solutions because they haven't yet learned to resolve conflict through reasonable and peaceful means.

For me, the problem became even more acute after I left Green Gulch. As I've already said, the families of the children at my new school were, by and large, a lot wealthier than my family. Coming from Green Gulch, I would have been perceived as something of a misfit in the best of circumstances, but because I was also looked upon as socially inferior, I found myself on the receiving end of almost relentless bullying and teasing. I might have been the tanto's kid at Green Gulch, but these kids didn't know that, and it probably wouldn't have impressed them in any case. Here I was not only an outsider and "different," I was also, from their point of view, "less than" they were.

At that time, I still maintained ties with the Green Gulch kids, and whenever we got together they invariably asked me about my new life. It had been several years since Julian's "war," Julian and his family had left Green Gulch, and I'd finally worked and sometimes bribed my way back into the other kids' good graces. So, when they heard about my being picked on, Dion, Micah, and Sean offered to go over to my new school and beat up my tormentors.

Until that year, we'd all gone to public school together. None of us had been picked on there, but we did stick pretty much to ourselves. In fact, on those few occasions when I tried to make friends with some of the other kids, it was my Green Gulch schoolmates who teased me about it. Now, whatever tensions might have remained among us, I was still a member of their tribe, and I think, in some way, they felt that by rejecting me, those kids were insulting them, too.

In the end, I refused their offer. On a philosophical level, I really did believe in the pacifist ideals I'd been taught. But also, on a practical level, I knew that my Green Gulch friends would go home after the fight while I'd be left to face my classmates the next day. I was old enough by then to understand that actions have consequences.

In some ways, there were similarities between the world of the Green Gulch kids and the world of my private-school classmates, but there were also some very fundamental differences. Both worlds were insular and intolerant of outsiders. But we at Green Gulch didn't consider ourselves superior to others. Rather, it was our sense of tribalism, which came from living in an insular community, that created our suspicion of outsiders. The children at my new school, however, considered themselves not only different from, but also superior to, me.

When I was a child, it was often hard for me to understand why the adults wanted me to be a pacifist. It sometimes seemed that they were telling me not to defend myself. And so, as I grew up, I began to think about how to defend myself and maintain my self-respect without at the same time wandering down the path of delusion, fear, anger, and hatred. Do I fight back, either literally or figuratively, and thus stand my ground? Do I sacrifice my own needs in order to keep the peace? Or is there some middle way? If I keep up my end of the conflict and raise my voice in response to someone who's raised his voice to me, if I insult someone who's insulted me, or use physical violence against a physical assailant, I might resolve the conflict, but at the price of hurting the other person.

It's a fundamental tenet of Buddhism that everything happens for a reason, and so, before we can make any kind of judgment, we must first try to determine the reason behind the situation or action we are judging. It would be easy to say simply that anger, hatred, and violence are bad, but a more profound understanding of the Buddhist teaching would be to understand that all these feelings have origins, even if they aren't good origins. Therefore, we try not to label someone's actions either "good" or "evil" without first trying to understand the reason for those actions. In a conflict, the other person might not see things from my point of view. He or she might not understand that I feel threatened. I might not be justified in doing whatever I do, even if I think I am. How do I know that I haven't inadvertently done something to make this person angry with me? And how can any of these questions be answered?

Certainly, in many cases, simple communication will resolve the disagreement, assuming both parties are willing to listen. But sometimes one person really does intend to harm the other, and no amount of communication will defuse the situation. What does one do then? At Green Gulch, the adults may have done a pretty good job of teaching us the principles of nonviolence, but they didn't do much to help us learn how to resolve conflicts when they arose.

• • •

In Buddhism we also believe that actions beget actions. This means that every time a person does something that affects someone else, that person will do something in response. That response is in itself an action and will likely cause a reaction from the first person. This can very quickly create a cycle of action and reaction in which two people keep doing things to each other with no end in sight. In the case of bad actions, if Person A does something hurtful to Person B, and Person B responds by hurting Person A, the two will soon be in a fight. A good Buddhist would find a way to break this cycle, or, better yet, to prevent its occurring in the first place. Knowing this, I've had to ask myself whether this teaching means that I should always turn the other cheek, or whether it means something else. Do I really have to be a pacifist in order to be a good Buddhist?

Just this past year, I had an encounter with the man in the apartment below mine. He liked to blast his music so loud that I couldn't relax at home. One day, the walls shook, the floor pounded, and my whole apartment was filled with the rumble of his bass.

I went downstairs and rang his bell. "Who is it?" a deep voice yelled from behind the closed door.

"It's Ivan, from upstairs," I yelled back, trying not to sound hostile while making myself heard over the music. "Could you turn it down?"

The door opened to reveal a hulking guy in boxers and an undershirt, his face just inches from mine. "The next time you come down here," he bellowed, "I'm gonna punch you right in the face!"

I took a step back and crouched, one foot in front of the other, as I'd been taught in aikido. "Jesus, man," I said, "your music's just really loud. All I'm asking you to do is turn it down."

The man stared at me for a moment before turning back into his apartment and slamming the door behind him. Over the next few days, he blasted his music just as loud as always. Finally, I called the building manager and explained the situation. She said she'd talk to the man and, a few days later, the music stopped.

I'd gone down there to try to work things out peacefully and reasonably. But, despite my best intentions, my neighbor had threatened me. When that happened, I believe, I'd had to stand my ground. My method of defending myself was not to threaten him back, which probably wouldn't have done much good considering the difference in our size, but to ask the manager to intervene. I do believe in nonviolence, but I also believe that I have to find a way to stand up for myself and my principles when the need arises.

In fact, I believe that learning to defend oneself actually makes one a better pacifist. Not being afraid means that one doesn't start down the road from fear to anger, anger to hatred, and hatred to violence. As kids at Green Gulch, we didn't have that kind of inner strength, which is why we fought so much. But as an adult, I see myself as a practical pacifist. I don't believe in war. I try not to create conflict. I try to avoid hurting others. I try to see both points of view in an argument, but I won't sacrifice myself simply to maintain peace.

FINDING THE MIDDLE WAY

I think now that the issue of nonviolence versus violence is more complicated than the Buddhists of my parents' generation thought. The adults at Green Gulch were, no doubt, influenced by the Vietnam War, and their view of Buddhist pacifism was very similar to the notions of pacifism shared by many of the people who'd been involved in the antiwar movement. My view, however, is different. But it's not simply the opposite of theirs; I think it's subtler than that.

I don't know if I'd say I'm a pacifist, but I try to be a good Buddhist, and as a good Buddhist I believe that actions do beget actions. I also realize, however, that there will be times when people do things that are hurtful to me and that negotiation won't always resolve the problem. At those times, I'm not prepared to be a martyr. Maybe an enlightened sage would always turn the other cheek, but I'm just a rank-and-file Buddhist. I believe I should always try to find a resolution through communication and negotiation, and that I should try to understand the other person's point of view. But I also believe that, when those tactics fail, I need to take whatever action is necessary to protect myself.

I would certainly never initiate any kind of physical violence, but, in the case of a physical assault, I believe I must do whatever it takes to keep myself from harm. This might mean fighting back, but it might also mean simply walking away, if that's a viable option. As I've explained, however, I don't think all violence is necessarily physical. Bullying, verbal abuse, and harassment are also forms of violence. And I believe that anyone who's the victim of that kind of nonphysical violence also needs to protect himself or herself, which might mean putting his or her own needs before the needs of another.

A saint or the Buddha might try always to do what's best for both parties, and might, therefore, never put himself or herself before another. But I don't believe that kind of self-sacrifice always works in the real world—certainly not for the average practitioner of any religion. Most of us who aren't saints or Buddhas must, when all else fails, do what we have to do in order to protect ourselves both physically and emotionally. And sometimes that means putting our own needs before those of the person who's trying to hurt us.

It's been a long road for me, but I've finally concluded that what the Buddha said about the Middle Way applies to the issue of nonviolence versus violence. I believe that the true Buddhist teaching is that it's important not to be controlled by destructive emotions like anger and hatred, which cause us to hurt the people with whom we share this planet, but, at the same time, I believe we have to defend ourselves when others are trying to hurt us.

EIGHT

EASTERN VERSUS WESTERN MORALITY

When I first started at Reed College in 1992, my fellow fresh-men and I often found ourselves, as I imagine most college students do, gathered in one dorm room or another discussing "weighty" and "important" issues. One of those issues revolved around our views on morality. Many of the other kids, who'd been raised in the Judeo-Christian tradition, appeared to con-sider the concepts they'd grown up with premodern, irrational, and no longer applicable to their everyday lives. In fact, they weren't terribly fond of the concept of morality in general. I disagreed with their view then, as I do now, probably because of the strong sense of morality with which I was imbued dur-ing my years at Green Gulch and afterward as a practicing Buddhist. To me, the Buddhist concept of morality is perfectly rational and just as applicable now as it was when the Buddha conceived it.

All religions, including Buddhism, are based on a strong

sense of morality, but Buddhism, which originated in India, is based on an Eastern concept of morality, which is very different from the moral concepts of the West.

Before I describe my understanding of Eastern morality, however, I think it's important to define what I mean by Western morality. If you think about it, there are really two kinds of Western morality: Judeo-Christian morality and what I think of as the modern Western perspective on morality.

TWO APPROACHES TO WESTERN MORALITY

Judeo-Christian morality is based on commandments from God—thou-shalts and thou-shalt-nots. It's based on the idea that good and evil are polar opposites, that God has clearly defined for man what is good and what is evil, and that he has commanded human beings to be good.

To some people, being good means strictly following scripture, although, of course, not every member of the Judeo-Christian population follows scripture or even cares about it. Those who don't look to the Bible for their definition of good and evil—the Quakers, for example—believe in a personal relationship with God, and base their concept of morality on what He communicates directly to them. But, there's yet another approach to morality in the West. In modern times, a lot of people don't care about God, scripture, or religion. Many people are not religious at all, and these people often ask the question, "How can anyone know which religion, if any, is right?" They—like many of my fellow students—don't believe that the Judeo-Christian notions of God, commandments, and doing good are concepts that apply in the modern world. These people would point to the fact that the Nazis also had a list of things they thought were good and things they thought were bad. The Nazis thought people of the Aryan race were good and that Jews, Gypsies, gays, and other people whom they sent to the concentration camps were bad. They killed millions of people in the Holocaust acting on that belief.

While I certainly understand that those who point to crimes against humanity as a reason to do away with all prescribed lists of good and evil wouldn't ever equate such man-made "commandments" with those handed down by a Judeo-Christian deity, they would, I believe, still point to the possibility for perversion that exists when one adheres to *any* list of preconceived dos and don'ts.

And they might further point out that if one starts from the rational assumption that there *is* no God, one can only conclude that human beings created all scripture in the first place. The Jews created the Old Testament. Early Christians created the New Testament. Muhammad created the Quran. Seen from that perspective, the moral codes espoused in these holy books reflect either the culture they came out of or the moral beliefs of the people who wrote them. And so, once again they would ask, "Who gets to decide what's good and what's bad?"

If you subscribe to one person's list, they argued, you might be like Mother Teresa, but if you subscribe to another's you might be like Hitler. And in any case, my college buddies would point out, many biblical concepts of what's "bad," "wrong," or "evil" simply do not hold up for most people in modern times.

The Bible, for example, states that homosexuality is wrong. As I understand it, many Christians have interpreted passages like Leviticus 19:22 or Romans 1:26–27 to be prohibitions against homosexuality, and stories like God's destruction of Sodom and Gomorrah as biblical evidence that God has declared homosexuality to be evil. There are also a number of biblical admonitions against sexuality in general, such as the passage in Deuteronomy 22:13–21, which says that if a man takes a wife and, after lying with her, slanders her by saying she was not a virgin, the woman's parents shall bring proof of her virginity to the town elders, and, if they do that, the girl's husband will be fined and he will be required to remain married to her for the rest of his life. But if the parents can't prove she was a virgin at the time of her marriage, she will be brought to her father's house and the men of the town will stone her to death.

Paul's Letters to the Apostles also abound with admonitions against sexual impurity or licentious behavior. A trained theologian or biblical scholar could probably rattle off many such references, of which the following from 1 Thessalonians 4:2–8 is just one:

For you know what instructions we gave you by the authority of the Lord Jesus. It is God's will that you should be sanctified: that you should avoid sexual immorality; that each of you should learn to acquire a wife in a way that is holy and honorable, not in passionate lust like the heathen, who do not know God; and that in this matter no one should cheat his brother or take advantage of him. The Lord will punish men for all such sins, as we have already told you and warned you. For God did not call us to be impure, but to live a holy life. Therefore, he who rejects this instruction does not reject man but God, who gives you his Holy Spirit.

So, my college peers, who didn't think there was anything wrong with homosexuality or premarital sex, not to mention sexuality in general, would argue that traditional Judeo-Christian concepts of what's good and what's evil no longer apply, and that it's, therefore, better for each person to determine for himself what's good and to act accordingly.

Although this approach seems fundamentally amoral to me, since it, effectively, jettisons the notion that there might be any objective way to determine right from wrong and gives anyone license to behave any way he wants, people like my fellow freshmen might have said that it doesn't necessarily preclude any particular individual from being a good person. At one extreme you might still have a Hitler, but at the other there would also be Mother Teresas. Or, in other words, having a predetermined list of what is good and what is evil doesn't mean there won't be people who choose to act in ways that are evil—and not having one doesn't mean there won't be people who choose to do good.

People who hold this view might feel that it's okay to do things for their own benefit, such as make a great deal of money, so long as they didn't hurt anyone else. Or they might, on the other hand, become politically active in a cause they felt was just and important. They might volunteer to work for a charity or donate money to help the poor. These people clearly would not be considered selfish, but their activism would come from a different place than it would for a person who ascribed to the Judeo-Christian view of morality. Those who espouse the modern Western view of morality might not believe in God, the afterlife, or that there's any higher cosmic meaning in the world, but that's not to say they wouldn't care about helping others. To these people, being moral might mean making the best of the world they live in.

So, I think the modern Western perspective on morality can be either moral or amoral, depending on how the individual applies it. If not believing in God or a higher power means to one person that it's okay to think only about him- or herself, I would consider that person amoral. But if to another it means making the best of the world we share, I think that person would be moral.

EASTERN MORALITY AND THE WHEEL OF KARMA

Eastern thought, however, takes a very different approach to morality than either the Judeo-Christian or the modern Western view. Buddhism is just one of many schools of thought in India and much of the rest of Asia, and so, before discussing Buddhist concepts specifically, I think it's necessary to talk a bit about Eastern concepts in general.

Eastern morality is not based on commandments from God or a higher power. It is not based on "thou-shalts" and "thou-shalt-nots." Much of Eastern morality is based on the concept of karma, which, as I've already explained, is simply the notion that actions have consequences. For purposes of discussion, I'll call this karmic morality.

Many Westerners appear to confuse karma with fate or destiny. I frequently hear people say things like, "Oh, man, I was really mean to somebody yesterday, and today I tripped over a stick and I thought, whoa, karma!" But karma doesn't mean fate or destiny at all. And there's nothing supernatural about it. In fact, the concept is very realistic, because people's actions really do have consequences.

In Buddhism, we commonly talk about the Wheel of Karma, meaning, as I said earlier, the cycle of actions and their consequential reactions. We discussed this concept as it applies to violence in the previous chapter. To use a very crude example, when one person punches another in the nose, and the second person's response is to punch the first person in return, a cycle of cause and effect is established. The only way to end the cycle is for one person or the other to stop reacting. As I've said, continuing to "turn" the wheel, so to speak, is called staying on the Wheel of Karma. Not reacting is called getting off the Wheel of Karma. Karma, as I've said, literally means "action" in Sanskrit, and, although it can also refer to the notion that actions have consequences in general, the term is often used to denote a specific action or reaction, in which case one can also speak of a person's karma as being a specific action he or she has taken or a specific reaction someone else has had to that action.

While certain types of karma—actions or reactions—can be labeled good or bad, the concepts of good and evil are not necessary to the Eastern view of morality. No particular action is considered intrinsically good or bad, and those adjectives would not be applied to karma until its consequences had been analyzed. Instead, the basic tenet of Eastern morality is that people must take responsibility for their own actions. Once that concept has been accepted, the various Eastern philosophies go off in different directions.

Although the Buddha argued in favor of getting off the Wheel of Karma, an argument could also be made for staying on the Wheel. In order to understand the Buddhist argument, it's necessary to first understand the counterargument.

If someone were arguing in favor of staying on the Wheel of Karma, he or she might say that we need to protect ourselves from those who wish us harm. In addition, if we didn't react, people would never have to face the consequences of their actions. And so, if someone tries to harm us, we should let him or her know his or her actions have consequences by doing something harmful in return.

This person might then argue that staying on the Wheel of Karma is moral, because no one would ever do anything harmful unless someone had done something harmful to him or her first. Moral people wouldn't harm anyone anyway, and immoral people would be less likely to do harm because they'd fear the consequences. It would then follow that, in a society where everyone knew their harmful actions would engender equally harmful reactions—or consequences—people would be less likely to initiate those harmful actions in the first place. No commandments would be needed to ensure moral behavior, just the fear of reactions.

The Buddha, however, disagreed with this argument. He believed we should get off the Wheel of Karma because, if we didn't, the cycle of action and reaction would continue to escalate endlessly. Seen from that perspective, staying on the Wheel of Karma is nothing more than taking revenge.

The Buddha thought there were alternatives to revenge, one of which is communication. If someone does something to harm you, you can try to find out why. Maybe you did, or are doing, something bad to him or her that you're simply not aware of. Maybe you're not doing bad things, but the person thinks you are. Maybe that person isn't even aware that he's hurting you or that you don't like what he's doing. In any of these cases, taking revenge would not only be an inappropriate response, according to Buddhist philosophy, it would also put you in the position of being the "bad" person, which means that you would be responsible for creating your own bad karma.

But what if the person who's hurting you really is doing it intentionally, even though you're not harming him or her in any way? Buddhist thought still holds that there are alternatives to revenge. One alternative would be simply to walk away from the situation. Another alternative would be to let the rest of your community know someone is doing bad things so that they could protect themselves from being hurt. And finally, it might be possible to protect yourself without actually hurting the person who is harming you. (Remember that one of the vows a Buddhist monk takes is, "A disciple of the Buddha does not bear ill will.") Finding any one of these alternatives would allow you to get off the Wheel of Karma.

Getting off the Wheel of Karma also requires finding the reasons behind people's actions. As I've already explained, Buddhism holds that whatever we do, we do for a reason. Perhaps a person is doing something harmful simply out of ignorance, or perhaps he or she really is greedy, selfish, jealous, hateful, or what have you. In Buddhism, however, we believe that people are not inherently good or evil. It's their actions that are good or evil, and they must take responsibility for those actions. Because of that, when a person does something we consider bad or harmful, we try to look for the cause of the action and fix the problem at its root, which would mean that the person no longer had any need to continue the action.

One non-Buddhist example of how karma works can be found in the biblical story of Cain and Abel. When Cain kills Abel, God asks, "Where is Abel?" Cain replies, "Am I my brother's keeper?" And God then asks, "What have you done?"

When God asks Cain where Abel is, Cain's reply, "Am I my brother's keeper?" puts up what we in modern times might call a red flag. You don't need to be omniscient to be suspicious of that response, because if Cain hadn't killed Abel, he'd probably just have said, "I don't know," and left it at that.

Cain's answer indicates that he is not willing to take responsibility for his action, but God doesn't immediately punish him for his fratricide. Instead, he simply asks the question, "What have you done?" To me, God appears to be trying to find out the reason, or root cause, for Cain's behavior and to make him take responsibility for his actions. Of course, I realize that to Jews and Christians, this story will have other implications, but it always makes me think of karma.

When I was in college, I didn't make the connection between my sense of morality and my Buddhist upbringing, but, looking back, I believe it was my concept of Eastern morality that prevented me and my college friends from communicating clearly with one another. They thought, naturally enough, that I was talking about Judeo-Christian morality—since that's all they knew—when in fact I was considering morality from a karmic point of view.

To this day, my sense of morality is very Eastern. Although I agree with the other students' view of the Nazis, I would approach the question of good and evil quite differently. I don't believe that just because one group of people created their own perverse list of dos and don'ts, we'd be better off replacing those lists with no moral code whatsoever. Rather, I would look to karmic morality and analyze the consequences of the Nazis' actions. Having done that, I can determine that their actions were bad, because they had bad consequences.

While I respect Judeo-Christian morality, I don't believe that any specific action can be termed inherently good or bad until we examine its consequences. In fact, there are several specific biblical prohibitions with which I would respectfully disagree. I don't believe that being gay, having premarital sex, or worshiping idols is immoral because, from a karmic perspective, none of these behaviors has any bad consequences.

There are, however, problems inherent in Eastern morality that I've needed to sort out for myself. For example, one person who I believe was almost as evil as Hitler is Charles Manson. In the 1960s, he encountered Zen and other schools of Eastern thought, and his rationalization for his heinous murders was derived from an extremely perverted view of Eastern concepts. When one practices Zen meditation, as I've explained, one goes into a state of mind where opposites no longer exist. Zen Buddhists do this in order to have a better understanding of the world. But Charles Manson reasoned that if there are no opposites, there can be no good or evil, and he used that reasoning to justify killing. When I think about what he did, it sometimes makes me question my religion. If I practice Zen meditation long enough, I sometimes wonder, will I too lose my sense of right and wrong? Fortunately, when I've wrestled with this issue, Buddhist thought has once more come to my aid.

One has only to look to the monks' vow, "A disciple of the Buddha does not willfully take life," to know that Charles Manson's perverted view is not the Buddhist view at all. But, if one wants to understand *why* Zen Buddhist monks take a vow not to kill, one has to go deeper into Zen Buddhist philosophy.

Zen meditation is an example of what the Buddha meant by Right Meditation, which is but one branch of the Eightfold Path. In a meditative state, people might, indeed, be capable of both good and bad actions, because the dichotomy between good and evil disappears from their minds. However, the Eightfold Path also includes Right Mindfulness and Right Action.

Right Mindfulness means being as mindful as one can of everything in one's world. It means understanding the suffering of others. It means understanding the results of one's actions. It means recognizing when one is hurting others. It means realizing that every human being on this planet has a body, a mind, and a soul that is dear and sacred to him or her. Right Meditation is supposed to help Buddhists have a better sense of mindfulness. Right Mindfulness and Right Meditation are supposed to complement each other as all of the branches of the Eightfold Path are supposed to complement one another.

From a Buddhist point of view, then, Charles Manson did not practice Right Mindfulness, nor did he follow Right Action, which means taking responsibility for one's actions and is essentially equivalent to the Buddhist view of karmic morality. In effect, Manson was refusing to take responsibility for his actions by saying, "Am I my brother's keeper?" The question I'd like to put to anyone who perverts any moral philosophy, Buddhist or otherwise, to rationalize doing evil is, "What have you done?"

In the end, I know that any moral system can be perverted to evil ends, and that, as a Buddhist, I am, therefore, on safe moral ground.

There's another moral issue, however, that for me hits far closer to home, and that's how the members of our community reacted to Richard Baker's corrupt activities. As I now understand it, despite several warning signs that a lot of people in the community should have noticed, no one took any action against him for a very long time. My father, for example, did the bookkeeping at the Zen Center for quite a while, and he had questions about Baker Roshi's management of Zen Center funds. In fact, he's told me that he had several talks with Baker about this and that Baker always came up with an explanation that sounded reasonable at the time but that later proved to be troubling.

I think the real problem at the Zen Center was that the adults were naïve. When I've asked him about what happened, my father has told me that he didn't necessarily trust Baker but he did trust Suzuki, who had chosen Baker to be his successor just before he died. And, my father said, because he trusted him, he believed that Suzuki must have had a good reason for his choice. In retrospect, he now concedes that

Suzuki, great Zen master though he was, might have had flaws just like the rest of us, and maybe one of them was being a poor judge of Baker's character.

After the community finally *did* take action and forced Baker to resign, many of the Zen Center people were outraged. Quite a number of changes have been made in the way the Zen Center governs itself as a result of the Baker scandal. As I understand, since my family left, the Zen Center has become more democratic in an effort to avoid being under the power of charismatic and corrupt leaders like Baker.

However, although this was the reaction of the majority of Zen Center people, to this day there are people who believe that we should just "meditate through" the issue. I think these people felt that by getting angry, they'd be staying on the Wheel of Karma, and that, according to the Buddha, they should be getting off. As a result, to this day, there are meetings of Suzuki's disciples to which Richard Baker is invited.

FINDING THE MIDDLE WAY

When it's a question of choosing between Eastern and Western morality, for me there can be no Middle Way. I'm a Buddhist, and my moral code is based upon Eastern philosophy. The real issue then becomes, within the confines of that philosophy, what action I should take in any given situation.

Let's say, for example, that I find out someone is corrupt or willfully hurting me or people I know. Assuming that person is neither acting illegally—in which case there wouldn't be any question but that I'd go to the police—nor engaging in physical brutality, what should I do? Should I just walk away? Should I confront the person and tell him or her to stop? What if he didn't stop whatever he was doing? Should I threaten him? Should I tell other people who were also in danger of being hurt? Should I try to organize other members of my community to take action against him? Should I make his actions public so that he won't have the opportunity to do it again?

The real question I have to ask myself is whether I believe in staying on the Wheel of Karma or getting off it. And, if I believe in getting off, as I should if I believe in Buddhism, what actions can I take that would allow me to get off without being either naïve or apathetic?

What if I'm merely suspicious but don't actually have proof that this person is doing anything wrong? I believe that if I question him or her and receive a less than satisfactory response (such as "Am I my brother's keeper?"), that should be reason enough for me to become concerned.

I would then begin to investigate the person's actions for myself, and, once I'd gathered enough information to be convinced of his or her corruption, I could ask him or her, "What have you done?" I don't think that's a naïve question because it implies that the person has done something wrong and needs to take responsibility for his or her karma.

At that point, I might take any one of the various actions mentioned above. Fortunately, the Eastern notion of karma can help me to analyze my choices. Should I walk away? Well, there'd be no harm in doing that if it were an option.

Should I confront the person? Yes, as I've already said, I believe that would be a right course of action. He or she might get angry and might act accordingly, but if he were really corrupt, I'd be right to ask, "What have you done?"

Should I threaten him or her? Well, normally I'd say no. I don't think there's anything constructive to be served by making threats. There's a difference, however, between threatening in a vengeful way and warning someone that you'll take action if he or she doesn't stop hurting you or other people. So, I think I'd be entitled to tell the person that continuing his or her course of action would have serious consequences.

Should I tell other people in the community? Absolutely. They'd have a right to know. Should I organize the community to take action? Again, yes. If I truly believed he or she were corrupt and had evidence to support my belief, I think I'd have a responsibility to take part in such a movement. The community, of course, might decide not to do that, in which case I could still make the person's actions public in an effort to prevent him from hurting other people. I think I would have an obligation to do that, because if I didn't, I'd be turning a blind eye and facilitating his or her behavior.

These choices, I hope, illustrate the balance I've been able to find between staying on the Wheel of Karma and being naïve. Following the course of action I've just outlined wouldn't be naïve, but it wouldn't necessitate my staying on the Wheel of Karma either. I wouldn't actually be harming the person by telling others what he'd done. In effect, he'd be harming himself because he would be forced to accept the consequences of his own actions. Finding this balance is the Middle Way.

• • •

To me, morality means two things. First, it means that I need to take responsibility for my actions. And second, it means that if other people aren't willing to take responsibility for theirs and are hurting me or people who are close to me, I need to take some action that will cause them to face the consequences and prevent them from causing further harm. That doesn't necessarily mean I have to hurt them in return, and it certainly doesn't mean taking revenge.

Thinking about how I might respond to bad and hurtful actions without hurting the other person and taking revenge, I've come to the conclusion that truth can be a powerful weapon. In the story of Cain and Abel, for example, God doesn't allow Cain to hide from the truth of what he's done. Immoral people don't want us to know they've done anything wrong, because they don't want to accept the consequences of their actions. So, I believe that bringing the truth out into the open not only forces them to accept responsibility for what they've done, it also brings their corruption to the attention of other people.

I don't think that taking action to protect yourself or others from harm means that you have to stay on the Wheel of Karma. The key, I believe, is to act without being vengeful. If you have enough mindfulness and enough information to know that someone is doing something wrong, telling other people doesn't mean you are staying on the Wheel of Karma.

Of course, as I've said before, I'm neither a hero nor a wise man. I'm just one person trying to understand my religion and make the best moral decisions I can. It's easy for me to talk about these things in theory, but it's quite another to actually practice what I preach, and I have yet to be tested. While I truly believe what I say about acting with mindfulness, it's another thing to understand what's going on in my world. But, if I can take responsibility for my actions, hold people to the truth of theirs, try my best to be mindful of the world around me, and keep my ego in check, I'd like to think I can be a reasonably moral person.

NINE

SILENCE VERSUS NOISE

One day when we were living at Green Gulch—I must have been about six or seven—I asked my mother if I could go into the zendo with her. I wanted to see what she and the others did in that place, which had always seemed so mysterious. She said I could, but I'd have to be very quiet. If I made any noise, I'd have to leave. I told her I'd be *very* quiet as long as I could be in the zendo with her.

I watched as she and the other adults walked over to the zafus and sat cross-legged or in the lotus position. A priest hit a gong three times. Its third ring sounded for a long time, taking, it seemed to me, forever to fade entirely. After that, everyone was silent. They just breathed slowly and calmly. They didn't move or talk. It wasn't even like school, where the students remained quiet and listened as the teacher taught a lesson. Here there was no teacher, only quiet students.

I tried to sit still, but I couldn't. It wasn't as interesting as I'd thought it would be. I don't know what I thought went on in the zendo. I guess I imagined the priests telling the adults secrets we children weren't old enough to hear. And I guess in a way that's what they did. They taught the students the secret of how to silence their minds.

I was *not* ready to understand that. I was glad to see what the adults did, but I couldn't get interested in silencing my mind. It was too full of curiosity. First I started to play with the cushions. Then I built a little fort. Finally, as I played with the pillows and mats in an effort to entertain myself, I began to hum. Everyone looked at me and then at my mother. My mother's breathing returned to its normal rhythm and she quickly escorted me from the zendo.

For someone who wasn't there, it may be impossible to understand the true silence of Green Gulch and the Zen Center. The best description I can think of is to compare it to the night, several years ago, when I took a hike under the full moon to a small beach that lay, washed up and down by the tide, in front of an amphitheater of cliffs. I was twenty and home from college for summer vacation with my parents, who now live in a house in the secluded hills at the edge of Mill Valley, California. Their house and the property around it is right on the border of some federally preserved land just outside of San Francisco called the Golden Gate National Recreation Area (or GGNRA for short). Under the government's protection, it remains undeveloped to this day, and the many hiking trails that weave through it are there to be enjoyed by San Francisco Bay Area residents. My parents' house is no more than a four-hour hike from the sea, and that night I had decided to make the hike by moonlight.

It was three-thirty in the morning. I could hear small animals in the bushes, but I was the only human on the beach. There were no beach balls, no radios, no children screaming or friends splashing one another. The surf's roar reverberating from the cliffs was the only sound apart from my own breathing. In the absence of any other noise, the ocean was so loud it seemed to fill the whole world. The awesome rumble was something like what I've always imagined a rock concert would sound like. If you can appreciate how quiet everything else must have been to make the waves sound so loud, you can imagine how quiet it was at Green Gulch, except without the waves. If you live in the country, perhaps on a farm, you might have experienced a comparable silence, but you'd never encounter anything like it in any urban area I know.

You may think it's quiet in your house or apartment when you're alone and you turn off your stereo, TV, and computer. But when I do that in my apartment, I can still hear cars driving by in the street. The neighbors still make noise. Someone else's TV is inevitably on. It's not nearly as quiet as the world of my childhood.

At Green Gulch, our whole world was ruled by silence. If you walked up through the fields toward the zendo, you would hear nothing but the minute rippling waves in our reservoir. Even around the Wheelwright Center, and in the residential area where my family lived in the Bullpens, it was just as quiet. If a gong rang, you could hear it from across the gulch.

If someone yelled, the sound would be broadcast like radio waves.

People always spoke quietly in the dining room. And even at home, where we could unwind and be totally ourselves, we kept our voices down. If someone did raise his or her voice, it would be only to what most of us consider a conversational level. That was usually sufficient to get other people's attention.

As different as this volume of life may seem to you, it was normal for me, and sounds that someone who didn't grow up at Green Gulch might find normal still seem loud to me.

The day my mother took me to the zendo, I learned my first lesson about the role meditation plays in Buddhism. I learned that it allows people to be totally still in both body and mind so that they can see clearly into themselves and thus become enlightened. When our mind is overstimulated or filled with noise, the waters of our consciousness are muddied, we can't think clearly, and we are blocked from enlightenment.

The silence at Green Gulch allowed the consciousness to remain clear. Even the chants spoke of silence. That passage from the Heart Sutra, for example, which I had childishly thought was describing a ghost, speaks of the way one who is enlightened can transcend the perceptions of his senses in order to "know things directly" and so avoid false conceptions. Any of the senses can betray us at any time—we may, for example, think we are seeing one thing when it is really another, or we might think we're hearing one word when it's really another with a similar sound—and so we may act inappropriately because we've been deluded by our senses. Transcending our senses allows us to act appropriately because we have a more enlightened understanding of reality. The point is that we shouldn't rely on our perceptions or preconceived notions but should try to come to a deeper kind of comprehension. Once we are able to do that, we'll have traveled some distance down the path to enlightenment.

Silence is one means we have of separating the self from the senses, and for that reason, it has come to symbolize, for me, the basic dichotomy between sensuality and asensuality.

Children, of course, love to make noise. They even seem, in some way, to need it. They encourage one another to make noise by tagging, tickling, splashing, hair-pulling, and squirting. Games almost always involve noise, whether counting in hide-and-seek or deciding who's "it" in tag.

We Green Gulch children probably made less noise than most, even when we got into fights. Most kids yell at or insult one another when they get angry. But we tended to fight or squabble silently, with shoving or quiet teasing. The problem was that we generally wanted to make *more* noise while the adults wanted us to make less. We were constantly being told to be quiet, and rules like "No Screaming in the Central Area" dominated our childhood. As a result, I'm still sometimes torn between a need for silence and a need to let out all that noise that was bottled up inside me. The Buddhist in me finds inner peace in tranquillity while the repressed kid wants to make all the noise I wasn't allowed to make in childhood. And yet, whenever I find that I want to make noise, I'm caught short by my old Green Gulch training. I have the paranoid feeling that I might be disturbing someone. Several times in my life, I've tried to yell at the top of my lungs, but I just can't do it. The sound I make always comes out something short of true, cathartic noisemaking.

No matter how noisy the adults at Green Gulch thought we were as children, however, our level of noisemaking was nothing compared to what I've found on the Outside. American culture is very loud. It's filled with noise. People listen to loud music. They give noisy parties. They honk their horns aggressively and yell to one another over great distances. They fill their homes with the noise of televisions, radios, and computer games. They put alarms on their cars and their houses, and except in a few of the most rural areas of the country, they live next to streets where cars drive by at all hours of the night. And even those who do live outside the cities and suburbs haven't been raised with a culture of silence, as I was.

When I entered middle school, which is when children generally go to their first school dances, I was scared, and not just because I was shy or afraid no one would want to dance with me. I was actually afraid of the noise. My first dance, I remember, was held in one of the larger classrooms. When I arrived outside the room, I could hear rock music pounding. Even from outside the door, it was too loud. It reminded me of all the things we weren't supposed to do at Green Gulch. We'd have gotten into *real* trouble if we'd made that much noise. When I finally got up enough courage to enter, the classroom was a sea of noise.

Ever since that experience, I've had trouble going to parties, and I think if the music weren't always so loud, I wouldn't have such a problem. It still amazes me how much of American culture revolves around loud noises. If Green Gulch was an asensual place, culturally speaking, America is its polar opposite.

Over time, I've come to think of silence and noise as metaphors for the dichotomy between everything I was raised with at Green Gulch and everything in the Outside World. Silence represents, for me, clarity of mind, calmness, and a simple lifestyle. Noise represents the cacophony of urban life and a mind that's cluttered and unenlightened.

When a television set is not tuned to any station, the random dots you see on the screen are sometimes referred to as "noise." Any time I see a group of random images, such as cars driving every which way or crowds in a shopping mall, I'm reminded of that kind of noise.

Bright colors can also be described as "loud." Green Gulch was a world of subdued tones dominated by the noncolors, black and white. The priests' robes were usually black, and if they weren't, they were brown. The zafus and meditation mats were also black. The buildings were either unpainted wood or aluminum siding. Our own house was brown and white.

The laypeople's clothing was practical and mainly in shades of blue, brown, gray, white, or black. Someone might wear a T-shirt that was incidentally yellow or a red-and-blue–checked shirt, but these items weren't chosen *because* they were colorful or flashy.

The Western world, however, is full of bright colors. Restaurants, places of entertainment, and storefronts glow with flashing neon signs. Almost any American city is just about the brightest thing I've ever seen at night. Buildings are lit up like Christmas trees; commercial establishments shine their advertisements in rainbows of light. Every street is illuminated and full of cars with lunar head beams. In all that brightness, you can't even see the stars.

Fashion is loud. From sequins to fluorescents to Britney Spears's outfit at the MTV Music Video Awards, fashion screams through the color spectrum like fireworks through the sky. In the late eighties, people wore bright-colored clothing in crazy patterns. In the nineties, it was purple, green, or blue hair. All these "loud" colors, for me, belong to the category of noise.

Maybe in earlier times, things were different. More people lived in the country where it was quiet and the world wasn't filled with bright colors or flashing lights. The stars were bright in the sky. And I'm sure there are still rural areas that are something like Green Gulch in the sense that they're relatively quiet, both literally and figuratively. But the noise, both actual and metaphorical, that I encounter every day has always been at odds with my upbringing. And, even as an adult, it has sometimes actually frightened or overwhelmed me. I remember, in particular, the one and only time I went to a nightclub where they were playing techno music. I could hardly process all the visuals. Lights were flashing and changing colors and turning on and off. One moment I saw everything and the next nothing. Or I might see my surroundings in white and then in red or blue, then in a combination of red and blue, and then in white again. Banks of TV screens along the walls and ceiling repeated dozens of computer animation videos I was supposed to "see" all at once. It was simply impossible for me to process such an assault on my senses.

It's not that I'm morally opposed to this kind of thing. It's just that a need for calm surroundings still runs deep within me. I think because I lived in that environment for the first ten years of my life, the need got hardwired into my brain.

FINDING THE MIDDLE WAY

For a long time, I tried to resist the hypersensuality of the Outside World. I didn't go to parties where loud music was played. I stayed out of bars and generally tried to be a good, calm Buddhist. I used to think non-Buddhists were just using noise to delude themselves and keep their minds from enlightenment.

Over the years, however, I've come to a better understanding of the human need for sensual stimulation and of the differences between my "native country" and this strange, new world I live in. I try to see myself as a citizen of the world, not just of Green Gulch, and when I do that, I can appreciate things like noise as an observer—up to a point. I still value tranquillity, but opening myself up to this hypersensual other country has allowed me to bring sensuality into my life.

By trying to look at American culture with an open mind, I'm attempting to resolve the conflict between silence and noise in my world. I believe that if Buddhism is going to continue as an American religion, American Buddhists will have to synthesize and balance their own values with those of American culture. We need to hold on to our belief in tranquillity and peace of mind while also accepting the noise in the rest of our world.

At Green Gulch, I could rely on the external silence to keep my mind clear. In America, I can't, because the noise is all around me. Sometimes meditation helps, but there are many times when I'm not meditating that I'm attacked by the hypersensuality I've come to associate with America. And sometimes the world around me is just too fast-paced for meditation to do me much good.

I'm not in control of the world around me, but I am in control of my mind. And I've learned to keep my mind quiet and clear in the midst of all that noise. If I can make my mind as silent as Green Gulch, I can keep it clear and remain focused even when the world around me is full of noise. Of course, I don't always succeed. But I try.

TEN

CONVERTS AND NATIVES

There's a difference between being a convert to a religion and being a native of that religion. A convert comes from a different religious background (or from no religious background at all) and decides to leave that old background to join the new religion. A native's religion comes from his or her background. A native was raised in that religion. It's not a choice made in adulthood but a part of his or her identity.

When my parents converted in the late 1960s, there were very few Buddhists in the West who were not of Asian descent. My parents and the other adults with whom I grew up at Green Gulch were pioneers. They all came from a Judeo-Christian, Western background. They explored the possibility of Buddhism in the West and made it a reality.

I, on the other hand, did not *find* Buddhism. I didn't have to reject or ignore any Judeo-Christian paradigm. I don't have a Western background to wrestle with. I didn't grow up as an insider to the West. I didn't approach Buddhism as an outsider. As a result, the converts of my parents' generation and the natives of mine have very different perspectives on Buddhism.

To me, the issue of converts and natives is not a conflict, because I am a native, not a convert, and I have a native's point of view—there's no conflict in my mind about that. But being a native has given me a very different perspective on Buddhism, and on religion in general, from what I believe most converts would have. And, for that reason, it seems to me that any discussion of who I am as a second-generation American Buddhist would not be complete without some explanation of what it means to be a native of my religion.

Several Christmases ago, just after I finished college, my parents practically dragged me to see the movie *Michael*. It was about the archangel Michael, who wanted to enjoy his last time on earth. According to the premise of the movie, angels get to return to earth only a certain number of times before they have to stay in Heaven forever. My parents thought going to the movie would be an entertaining family activity for the holiday season. But, for some reason I didn't quite understand myself, I didn't want to see *Michael*.

I told my parents I didn't want to go, but they were quite insistent. Since I couldn't give them a good reason for not wanting to see it, I finally gave in. My parents liked it. They thought it was a sweet movie about how many good things there are right here on earth rather than in Heaven, but I just couldn't relate to it.

After I'd had time to think about it, I was able to piece together my reasons for not wanting to see the movie and for not being able to enjoy it. I'd just spent four years away from my family. Of course, I'd come back to visit several times during those years, but college had changed me a lot. For one thing, leaving home had given me the distance, both physical and psychological, to reflect on my life at Green Gulch and my life with my parents outside Green Gulch. In fact, it was during this time that I began to think seriously about the conflicts I've been discussing here. Those conflicts had always been a part of my life, but it wasn't until I was away at college that I'd begun to consider them in any formal way.

Previously, when I'd celebrated Christmas with my parents, I hadn't given much thought to its being a Christian holiday. As I've said, our Christmas celebrations had always been more about Santa Claus than they were about Baby Jesus. In my reflections during college, however, I'd come to think about the significance of the fact that we as Buddhists were celebrating Christmas. I'd also come to realize how much I valued my Buddhist heritage. As a child, I'd never thought very much about the story of Baby Jesus, but as a young college graduate, I finally appreciated how important the story of the life of the Buddha, which was read to us at Buddha's Birthday, had been to me.

As a result, I think that when I saw *Michael,* I realized it simply wasn't part of my culture. The issue wasn't really that one had to be Christian to appreciate it, but rather that its storyline and message were based on a cultural understanding and acceptance of Judeo-Christian concepts like angels, God, and Heaven. Its intended audience was clearly those people who, whether or not they were practicing Christians or Jews, had grown up with the concepts upon which the movie was based. Heaven, God, and angels were all part of their cultural mythology, but not of mine.

Perhaps foolishly, I was surprised when I realized my parents didn't really understand why these concepts seemed so foreign to me. Even though they'd left Green Gulch, they still considered themselves Buddhists, so I thought they would have understood why I'd have trouble relating to a movie like *Michael*. I then realized, however, that even if they didn't actually believe in angels, they'd been raised in a culture where angels, literally or symbolically, were part of their heritage. They were comfortable with the cosmology of the Bible and had grown up on the myth that there are angels in Heaven. So, even without believing in Heaven, they found the story of *Michael* heartwarming.

Apart from the fact that I couldn't relate to *Michael*, my quarrel wasn't really with the movie itself. Rather, I was angry with my parents for insisting that I see it with them. For the first time I realized how different they were from me. I thought about it for a long time until I finally understood how big a difference there really is between converts and natives.

In addition to the converts of my parents' generation—and of mine—there is yet another category of Buddhist from whom I differ. These people may or may not be actual converts, but they come to Buddhism in search of what they call "spirituality." Spirituality can be a kind of religiosity that differentiates itself from any organized religion, or it can be a sort of religious buffet from which people are free to choose elements of Hinduism, Buddhism, Taoism, Native American religion, Islamic mysticism, and even elements of Judaism and Christianity, and combine them on their plate to create their own, customized belief system. There's nothing wrong with that, but for me Buddhism is the main course. Buddhism *is* my religion.

I take pride in being a second-generation American Buddhist. I'm proud to carry on the tradition started by my parents and others like them. I take my religion seriously. For me, it's more than simply a part of my background, as it might be for someone who didn't practice the religion he or she inherited more or less as an accident of birth. Buddhism has been an important influence on my life both as a child and as an adult, and I don't feel comfortable making it just one part of a generalized spiritual smorgasbord. Of course, people who prefer the spiritual buffet can be just as serious, but what they're serious about is different from what I'm serious about.

I admire those convert seekers of my parents' generation as well as my own. It takes a certain kind of courage and vision to leave the comfort of what one has known and look beyond one's inherited belief system in order to find something more fulfilling. And I understand that some people might prefer the spiritual buffet because they're suspicious of or uncomfortable with the concept of organized religion. But for me the quest is over. I'm comfortable both with the idea of organized religion and with the religion I inherited, and I don't feel the need to seek further. I'm only twenty-seven, and I realize that in the future many things might change, but for now, I've made the decision to stick with Buddhism, and I would hope that those who are still on their spiritual journey would also respect people like me.

• • •

There are, of course, many converts who have studied Buddhism for decades, who have become teachers and masters, and who've even become ordained priests, as my father did. They are the leaders, teachers, and elders in the Buddhist community, and they know a lot more about Buddhism than I do. But many of those people tend to describe Buddhism as a nonlogical religion, which is what drew them to it in the first place. I, on the other hand, don't see Buddhism as nonlogical. If, for example, the Four Noble Truths state that life is suffering, suffering is caused by desire, suffering is overcome through the cessation of desire, and the cessation of desire is achieved through enlightenment, that is a perfectly logical progression. The fact that we all suffer is a strong first principle, and from there the rest can be argued.

In fact, theistic religions that are based solely on faith seem, to my mind, more nonlogical than Buddhism. The Ten Commandments are not statements of logic but ultimatums handed down from God on high. They are not beliefs to be argued over with logic but, to the believer at least, facts and laws that are true not because they can be proved or because they stand upon first principles but simply because a "higher power" has *said* they are true.

I think the reason Buddhist converts describe Buddhism as nonlogical is that they grew up with Western philosophy and maybe Christian theology, and, for that reason, they think only in terms of Western logic. I, however, grew up comfortable with Eastern ways of thinking. To me, meditation is a form of experience and, therefore, a type of metaphysical empiricism. When I was trying to decide whether or not I believed in the concept of the soul, for example, I meditated. I went into the meditation knowing the modern argument from biology that we are just the sum of sensory input and chemical emotions. But when I cleared my mind of conscious thought and emotion, it seemed to me that I was still conscious, despite a lack of reaction to stimuli. As a result of that experience, which I understand to be an empirical truth, I came to conclude that consciousness is, in itself, neither stimulation nor reaction, and that it is, therefore, something separate from the biological explanations of input and output. For that reason, I believe in the soul. That's not Buddhism, it's just my opinion, but the point is that I got there by building logic upon a meditative foundation. It's not Western logic, but it's logic.

Another issue—also related to the use of logic—on which my perspective is different from those of most of the converts I know revolves around the hierarchical system, according to which more senior practitioners or teachers are considered to be wiser and closer to enlightenment than junior practitioners or students, so that the more junior practitioners are expected to take the teachings of their seniors virtually on faith.

In Zen, there has traditionally been a very strict master/student relationship in which the student is expected to be subservient to the master, almost in the same way an apprentice in medieval Europe would have served the artisan master to whom he was indentured. As my father has explained it to me, this tradition really springs more from the Chinese and Japanese cultures in which Zen originated than it does from Buddhism itself, and, in fact, it's a tradition that's become somewhat diluted in this country, where it really runs counter to the American culture. Nevertheless, even when Baker Roshi was the abbot of the San Francisco Zen Center, his students took on a fairly subservient role.

By now it should be clear that this tradition can become problematic when the leader's motivations are less than pure. And, in fact, since Baker Roshi's resignation, the San Francisco Buddhist community has, to a degree, modified the tradition. Students, for example, no longer refer to their teachers as "masters," but, in my opinion, they still seem to take their teachers' "teachings" too much on faith.

And, perhaps as a result of their not being questioned, too many teachers seem to convey their teachings in rather vague terms. When I attend lectures that include a question-and-answer period, I rarely hear the students asking the kinds of intellectual, logical questions that I think would cause the teacher to clarify his points. While I certainly respect these teachers and fully realize they have a much deeper understanding of Buddhism than I, I still believe that American Buddhism would benefit if they were encouraged to be more specific in their teachings.

The way to achieve this, I think, is through respectful, logical debate or the kinds of discussions that university students and their professors engage in as a matter of course. There are certainly people who would say that I'm not qualified to suggest this type of change since I'm not a Zen master myself, and perhaps they're right. But, having been raised with Eastern logic, I do bring a perspective to the issue that even the most senior convert may not have. And if, as I understand it, Buddhism in India, its birthplace, was far more intellectual than it is in China or Japan, perhaps my suggestion is not so radical as it might at first appear.

Clearly, any such debate would have to be based upon the Eastern intellectual tradition, and would include concepts such as meditation, but I believe it would be healthy for the Buddhist community if students, through questioning and discussion, were better able to determine for themselves what *they* think the Buddha really meant by one teaching or another.

The ability to question, as well as problem-solve through the application of logic and intellect, is far more compatible with the American way of thinking than the more poetic Chinese or Japanese approach. And it seems to me that if Buddhism is to survive and thrive in America, it would do well to adapt, as have other religions throughout time, to the culture in which it's being practiced.

It should be clear by now that I believe one of the areas in which my parents' generation failed is that it neglected to prepare the new generation—mine—to carry on the tradition they'd founded. I hope to learn from their mistakes by looking to the future. If American Buddhism is here to stay, not only will there be more converts and more natives born into it, but also there will be changes in the religion itself as it is more and more integrated into the American culture.

To all future converts, I say, "welcome." If Buddhism is only one piece of your spiritual quest, I hope it helps you to find what you seek, but if it's your "main course," there's nothing wrong with considering it your religion. In either case, my advice, for what it's worth, would be to study the sutras, practice meditation, respect the people who know more about Buddhism than you do, but also feel free to use the Eastern logic it's based upon to analyze its teachings for yourself and, as I hope, find the answers you've been seeking.

And finally, if you're a Buddhist who has children, or if others in your congregation have children, I would ask that you welcome those kids as young Buddhists. Teach them about their religion. If they're curious about what you do in your practice, let them into your meditation hall to see what you do. Understand that they'll grow up as Buddhists. They may stay with Buddhism as I have, or they may reject it, but whatever their decision, you need to know that your Buddhist practice will have a profound effect on their development and, above all, you should keep in mind that they may very well grow up to become the next generation of American Buddhists.

FINDING MYSELF

I still practice Buddhism today. I have a zafu that I sit on to meditate. I have an altar with a Buddha statue and an incense burner with sandalwood incense. I regularly attend the Berkeley Zen Center. Mel Weitsman, the abbot, is a disciple of Suzuki, and the Berkeley Zen Center still maintains a loose affiliation with Green Gulch and the San Francisco Zen Center.

Green Gulch still exists. As I've said, it still operates as a center for Zen Buddhist practice, but it's no longer a commune, and at the time of this writing most of the people who go to Green Gulch live off campus. I still stay in touch with some of the old Green Gulch people and I'm still friendly with some of the other Green Gulch children. But, I'm not really a Green Gulcher anymore; I'm my own person living in America.

• • •

Whether or not one is a Buddhist, I believe the first step toward enlightenment is finding oneself. I'd like to think that working through the conflicts I've been discussing here, weighing the two sides of each, one against the other, and deciding which carries more weight for me, has helped me to understand my own identity.

One thing I've found out about myself is that I'm an observer. Earlier, I talked about going to the millennial New Year's Eve celebration in San Francisco. I'd never been to a conventional New Year's Eve celebration before, and I went that year mainly to see what it was like. I observed. After all, isn't that part of Buddhism too, in a way? We Buddhists seek not God or righteousness but enlightenment. And, in order to become enlightened, don't we need to understand the world around us?

As I've also said, I didn't enjoy the event (or its aftermath). The experience did, however, help me to understand myself as a square peg who's not going to fit into a round hole. But, maybe everyone's a square peg at some time in his or her life, depending on the situation. Understanding that there are times when everyone will be a square peg in a round hole is a form of enlightenment, and when I see that clearly, all my frustrations about not fitting into American culture abate and I can breathe easy.

I now realize I don't fit in because people don't understand me. But it's not other people's fault they were raised more traditionally than I, nor is it mine that I wasn't. I'm just different.

I've struggled long and hard with the conflicts in my life, and the difficulty, as I now see it, arose not just from my feeling at odds with America, but as a result of my realization that I was also at odds with some aspects of my life at Green Gulch. Had the lines of battle been more clear-cut, perhaps the struggle would have been easier. As I've come to understand it, however, what I've done in some small way, and on a much smaller scale, mirrors what the Buddha did in his life.

The Buddha's quest for enlightenment began, as did mine, when he left home, the palace where he'd grown up. At first he sought the opposite of being rich by practicing with the ascetics, but he finally weighed the self-imposed poverty and self-denial of the ascetics against the luxury and indulgence of the palace and found the Middle Way. I feel that, in my own, personal way, I've done something similar by weighing the opposites in my life, figuring out where I stand on each issue in order to determine what's really important in my life, and so taking one small step toward enlightenment.

I also believe that by comparing the culture I was raised in at Green Gulch to traditional American culture, I have come to understand who I am as a second-generation American Buddhist, and that by understanding my own identity I have gained some insight into where American Buddhism stands today as well as where it is headed in the future.

I imagine the average "mainstream" American would look at people like my parents and dismiss them simply as hippies. But I'm not a hippie. I'm not a Buddhist because I'm rebelling against the culture of my birth or because I left behind my native tradition to find something new. I believe that, living in America as a Buddhist, I'm as much a part of American culture as an American Christian or Jew.

At one time, long ago, a Buddhist monk named Bodhidharma brought Zen Buddhism to China (or so the legends say). There was some point when the Chinese had never heard of Buddhism. There was a time when the Thai and Vietnamese people weren't Buddhist. There was even a time when Buddhism was first carried up into the Himalayas to Tibet. Now it has come to America.

I don't believe it has come simply as a short-lived form of counterculture. I don't think it's being practiced on Western soil just as a fad or rebellion against Western religious traditions. The second generation, however small, is some proof of that.

There may not be many of us right now, but since the sixties Buddhism has become popular all over America and throughout Europe as well. Many new Buddhist centers with Western congregations have sprung up over the past three decades so that there is now a Buddhism that is native to our country and to the West. It's still just a baby. It may take a long time to grow, but I do know it's here.

Being a second-generation American Buddhist, however, central as it may be to my identity, is not entirely who I am. For me, thoughts about being a Buddhist are inextricably intertwined with thoughts about being the child of hippie parents. And, while most Americans of my generation weren't raised Buddhist, many were raised by parents involved in the counterculture of the sixties and seventies who would have been identified as hippies (quaint as that term may now sound). Any of these people, I think, would profit from the kind of self-exploration and reflection I've done in my own quest to understand my own internal conflicts and discover who I am.

One admonishment I keep receiving from members of the hippie generation—even though many of them are now briefcase-toting, commuting suburbanites—is that my generation ought to be rebelling against the "establishment," as they did. But if we were to do that, as our parents did, it seems to me that we wouldn't be any different from them.

I'm constantly being asked what my generation stands for and what we're doing *as a generation*. Members of the hippie movement stood for specific ideals, banded together around a common political stance, and voiced a generation-wide protest. And it seems to me that many of those same people, even though they themselves may have long since "sold out" to suburbia, would like my generation to do as they did in their own youth. They'd like us to be another generation of hippies.

But what if we don't agree with all their ideals? How can my generation differentiate itself from theirs? Our parents differentiated themselves from *their* parents' generation by rebelling, but, it seems to me, the only way we could rebel would be to embrace the traditions they themselves rebelled against, which would mean turning our backs on everything they'd worked for. So, what role *can* we play in our world? What new roads can we pave for the future? Is there something we can do that doesn't involve rebelling against tradition but doesn't require totally embracing it either?

Instead of being another generation of hippies, and instead of creating a backlash against their ideals, I think we can weigh both sides. Each one of us can figure out which elements of each side he or she wants to retain and which ones to jettison. Our role can be to decide for ourselves where the balance lies between traditional culture and counterculture. And, in doing that, each one of us will be able to find ourselves. We can start a new tradition—based on the balance we find—and chart a direction for the future. That isn't Buddhism, but it is finding the Middle Way.